Forever ME, Lucy AND THE LORD

A 30-DAY DEVOTIONAL

Don Hocker

Forever Me, Lucy, and the Lord
by Don Hocker

Copyright © 2025 by Don Hocker

All rights reserved.

Printed in the United States of America
ISBN: 978-1-962802-39-0

All rights reserved. Except in the case of brief quotations embodied in critical articles and reviews, no portion of this book may be reproduced, stored in a retrieval system, or transmitted in any form or by any means—electronic, mechanical, photocopy, recording, scanning, or other—without prior written permission from the author.

All Scripture quotations marked NIV are taken from THE HOLY BIBLE, NEW INTERNATIONAL VERSION®, NIV® Copyright © 1973, 1978, 1984, 2011 by Biblica, Inc.® Used by permission. All rights reserved worldwide.

High Bridge Books titles may be purchased in bulk for educational, business, fundraising, or sales promotional use. For information, please contact High Bridge Books via www.HighBridgeBooks.com/contact.

Published in Houston, Texas, by High Bridge Books.

I dedicate this book to God, my Creator; to Jesus, my Savior; and to the Holy Spirit, my Guide.

CONTENTS

Introduction — 1

Day One: Victory — 5
Day Two: Grace — 9
Day Three: The Tragedy Of Delay — 13
Day Four: The Incarnation Of Jesus — 19
Day Five: Praise To God — 23
Day Six: Mission Possible — 27
Day Seven: Giving Up Control — 31
Day Eight: Satan's Impostor — 35
Day Nine: Reservation In Heaven — 41
Day Ten: Perfection — 45
Day Eleven: Do The Right Thing — 49
Day Twelve: Jesus, Our Ark — 55
Day Thirteen: Salvation Lost? — 61
Day Fourteen: The Power of Words — 65
Day Fifteen: Send Me — 69

Day Sixteen: Heaven's Dew	75
Day Seventeen: Three Cups	79
Day Eighteen: Open Invitation	85
Day Nineteen: Wonderous Love	91
Day Twenty: It Ain't That Hard	97
Day Twenty-One: God's Family	101
Day Twenty-Two: Living In A Secular World	105
Day Twenty-Three: Death (And Then There Is Grace)	111
Day Twenty-Four: Our Amazing God	115
Day Twenty-Five: Thy Will Be Done	121
Day Twenty-Six: I Can Only Imagine	127
Day Twenty-Seven: The Ultimate Gift	133
Day Twenty-Eight: Trust In The Lord	137
Day Twenty-Nine: The Joy of a Relationship With Jesus	141
Day Thirty: Life And Legacy	145

INTRODUCTION

IF SOMEONE TOLD ME, "HEY, DON, YOU WILL START YOUR THIRD DEVOtional book in 2024," my initial response would have been like good ol' Doubting Thomas of the twelve disciples' clan: "I got to see it before I believe it." But here I am. After several months of preparation and topic and passage selection, I am at the keyboard on July 20, 2024, typing this introduction.

Writing these devotional books has been a journey I never would have imagined. Beginning with the first book in 2021[1] where I explained my faith journey in the introduction to the second publication in 2023[2] where I expressed, in the introduction, my gratitude for those who obtained copies of the first book and made generous donations for charity for the book. Now this one.

Please allow me to make some reflections on what I have learned over these past few years while publishing these devotionals.

First, God is good all the time! Man, He has truly blessed me in immeasurable ways. As I have stated before, I have a great family, great friends, and a wonderful job, and the list goes on. Be thankful, my friends, because God has blessed you too!

Second, life is very short. I find it hard to believe that I am at this stage of my life where retirement and Medicare are becoming a reality. It seems like just yesterday I was a student at Clemson, enjoying life (maybe too much) and never thinking about living life in 2025. If there was any advice I could give myself then, it would be what I want to say now: Make the most out of your life. Leave a lasting legacy.[3]

Third, Heaven is real. Eternity is real. Salvation is real. Our Heavenly Creator is real. Jesus is real. God's love is real. These are the true realities of life.

Fourth, humor should be a part of everyone's DNA. Life is tough. Life has many challenges. It is easy to stress over problems we have. Of course, to face life's trials and tribulations, we need to go to God first. After that, we need to experience some fun and humor. And more likely than not, that fun and humor are probably God's medicine for you. So, take a large dose.

Fifth, pray, pray, pray. Never let a day go by where you are not talking with God. Pray often. Short prayers. Long prayers. Eyes open or shut. On your knees or in your car.[4] Prayers of thanksgiving. Prayers of forgiveness. Prayers of adoration. Prayers of intercession. So much variety. The list is endless. The main thing is to stay connected to our Heavenly Father. Pray, pray, pray.

I sincerely hope that you enjoy this third devotional book that I have written. I continue to try and stay basic by simply focusing on what I believe to be important. I talk a little more about Heaven in this book than I did in my first two books. Maybe that is because I am getting closer to Heaven than I have ever been before. Well, I guess you are too. Heaven is forever, and I know that my Lucy (my precious dog) is in Heaven. Lucy and I in Heaven together—forever!

This day, and every day, is a day that the Lord has made. Always rejoice and be glad in it! Amen!

INTRODUCTION

[1] I actually started writing the first devotional book, *Just Me, Lucy, and the Lord*, when COVID-19 hit the United States in March 2020.

[2] *Still Me, Lucy, and the Lord*

[3] See "Day Thirty" devotion.

[4] I talked about this in my first book. praying in the car!

Day One

VICTORY

When the perishable has been clothed with the imperishable, and the mortal with immortality, then the saying that is written will come true: "Death has been swallowed up in victory." "Where, O death, is your victory? Where, O death, is your sting?"

—1 Corinthians 15:54–55 NIV

VICTORIES ARE A PART OF LIFE! WE HAVE VICTORIES IN SPORTING events, political races, and even in war. We have victories in our personal lives and in our public lives. Victories can be large or small. I have been victorious in remaining cancer-free since 2016 and am also victorious in now flying in an airplane with very little trepidation.

While I will come back to the above text, I would like to share a few other passages of scripture that deal with victory and what we can take away from these passages.

"May we shout for joy over your victory and lift up our banners in the name of our God" (Ps. 20:5 NIV). When we experience a victory, there is a joy associated with it, and we need to learn that there is tremendous joy that can only come from a relationship with our Lord.

"For the Lord your God is the one who goes with you to fight for you against your enemies to give you victory" (Deut. 20:4 NIV). Our enemies do not necessarily have to be adversaries in war but can be enemies from within, such as addiction, pride, greed, or really any sin for that matter. Also, there are those enemies from outside, such as ridicule, scorn, or rejection. Once again, it is God who is there to provide the victory.

"For everyone born of God overcomes the world. This is the victory that has overcome the world, even our faith" (1 John 5:4 NIV). It is by our faith in God that we achieve victory against everything this secular world throws at us.

So here is what we have: Joy in the victory, the victory is God-created, and the victory is the product of our faith. Let's tie this back into our main scripture passage from 1 Corinthians, which says in part, "Death has been swallowed up in victory." God sent Jesus to this earth to die for our sins. But, of course, God did not stop there. No, He did not—He went another big step forward. He brought His Son, Jesus, back to life three days later. That tomb Jesus was buried in could not hold Him. That big boulder at the entrance could not block Jesus from leaving that burial place. Yes, death no longer had a hold on Jesus, as God would not allow it. God defeated death for Jesus, and God defeats death for every Christian who has placed their faith in Jesus as Lord and Savior. We are victorious as Jesus is victorious! What a benefit of our faith in what God has done by providing life eternal in Heaven. Oh man! No more sin, no more illness, no more pain, and no more death. Now, there is joy in this beyond measure. To experience this assurance that there will be no more permanent death is exhilarating and simply amazing.

Now, we don't just have this future hope of salvation for all eternity. No, we want to celebrate it now. We want to celebrate the victory today. How do we do it? Let me first talk about how not to celebrate our victory, and I am going to pull an example from the field of sports. There is nothing more wrong, nothing more irritating to me than to see a young athlete "taunting" a player on the opposing team after a score or after a win at the end of the game. Just as bad as "taunting" is bragging with so much pride about an accomplishment on the field or court. I will tell you right now that this is not how Christians should celebrate our victory over death—full of boastful pride. Then, how do we celebrate it? We do it with a heartfelt and humble appreciation for what Jesus has done for us.

There are two great quotes I have come across concerning celebrations:

> Celebrations infuse life with passion and purpose. They summon the human spirit.[1]

> One should never, but never, pass by an opportunity to celebrate.[2]

We Christians should celebrate with passion and purpose, and we should never let an opportunity pass by without showing our joy in our victory, our faith in our victory, and our appreciation to our Lord in Heaven for what He has done.

As I am writing this devotional, I am reminded of that great hymn "Go Tell It on the Mountain."[3] We *should* go tell it on the mountain and not be shy. Let it be known that death is no longer an option! Let it be known that the grave is simply a temporary holding place for our physical bodies. Let it be known that life eternal is a reality for those who have faith. Let's make our celebration known to others. It will make a difference!

Thought: How does having victory over death and an eternal salvation in Heaven make you feel?

Let us pray: Heavenly Father, thank You for Your Son, Jesus, who went to the cross for me, and thank You too for bringing Him back to life so that because of His victory, I can be victorious as well. Amen.

---

[1] Terrance E. Deal, leadership expert and author

[2] J.D. Malouf, attorney

[3] My dad's favorite hymn!

Day Two

GRACE

For it is by grace you have been saved, through faith—and this is not from yourselves, it is the gift of God—not by works, so that no one can boast.

—Ephesians 2:8–9 NIV

THERE IS A LINE IN THE GREAT HYMN "PRAISE TO THE LORD, THE Almighty,"[1] which ends verse four like this: "Then to thy need God as a mother doth speed, spreading the wings of grace o'er thee." This line creates in my mind an image of God flying over all creation like a mighty eagle full of power and speed, showering His people with grace after grace after grace.

What is grace? The best definition I have, even though it may sound like a Sunday School answer, is this: the free, unmerited favor of God working powerfully in minds and hearts to change lives for the better.

Let's unpack this definition. The first thing we see is that grace is free. Hmm... Is there not always a catch to something when it is "free"? Maybe in this world, but not with God, and certainly not with God's grace. I am here to tell you it is as free as free can be. It costs absolutely nothing. Okay, free is good then.

Secondly, Grace is unmerited. You mean to say, "We cannot earn it"? Paul's passage from Ephesians in this devotional says no works. We do not earn it. We cannot even ask for it. We cannot even get down on our hands and knees and beg and plead for it. Nope, God is calling the shots on this one! We must be careful not to use God's grace to become entitled. Quite frankly, we must realize that we are awfully sinful folks, and to believe that we are in some way deserving or even worthy of what God has for us is not a smart position to have. It is like David believing he was strong and powerful enough to fight Goliath without help from God. It just would not happen without God.

So, with some idea of what grace is, I now want to talk with you about the two basic forms of grace. One is typically called common or sustaining grace, and that, my friends, is for everyone. Yes, everyone. It is God's love for us allowing us to breathe every few seconds of each day, having food on the table and a wonderful family to enjoy life with. God extends this Grace to those saved and unsaved. It is God's plan to make this grace real for everyone so they can realize their need for a Savior.

The other form of grace, and so wonderful it is, is saving grace. This grace is for the believer. It is the grace that God shared with His people when Jesus went to the cross to die for the forgiveness of our sins and the salvation of our souls. This is the greatest act of grace, hands down—no close seconds! God's love in perfect form.

I want to wrap up this discussion with why grace is so very, very, good, and I am here to tell you it is.

Grace is so very, very good because not only can we say Christ died for the world,[2] but we can also say Christ died for me, yes me!

GRACE

It makes it so much more personal to be able to say this, and when we come to that realization, then our relationship with our Lord and Savior becomes that much more real.

Grace is so very, very good because it teaches us about forgiveness. I am reminded of a true story in an Amish community in Pennsylvania. On October 2, 2006, around 10 a.m., a man by the name of Charles Roberts entered the West Nickel Mines Amish School heavily armed, and he killed five young students and wounded five others. He then killed himself. In an unbelievable showing of forgiveness, more than half of those in attendance at Roberts' funeral were those Amish people from the community where the school was located. Too, many of these same Amish people brought food to the Roberts family. This show of grace and forgiveness from the Amish community astounded the world. But they demonstrated something we should all realize. God's grace is all about forgiveness because He forgave us of our sins through Christ's death on the cross. When we realize that, we can become more forgiving of others.

Grace is so very, very good because it helps us handle the problems, trials, and issues that we face every day of our lives. Does God's grace say, "Oh, because you have faith, you will not experience any struggles today?" No! But what God's grace does say is, "I am going to give you the tools to handle that problem that has surfaced in your life. I am going to help you get through it." That is comfort, my friends.

Grace is so very, very good because it makes us more generous and grateful people. Jesus told us, "Freely you have received; freely give"(Matt. 10:8b NIV). Through prayer and meditation, we then realize how generous God has been, and we develop that desire within to show generosity to others. That gratefulness becomes the catalyst to "freely give" as Jesus instructed.

Grace is so very, very good because it is simply about God's love for us. That love is deep! That love is strong! That love never changes or wavers! That love is constant! It is amazing that God would love us as much as He does and then shower us with His grace, knowing all along just how utterly sinful we are.

So here is our charge today and every day. Once God's grace seeps into every facet of our being, we then need to strive to show more compassion, more kindness, more generosity, and more forgiveness to everyone.

Grace is amazing!

Thought: How can you meditate more on God's grace? What are ways you can demonstrate His grace in your life? What are ways you can see grace in your life?

Let us pray: Your Grace is amazing, Lord. Fill me every day with it so that I can share it with others through acts of compassion, forgiveness, kindness, and love. Amen.

---

[1] Hymn 139, *The United Methodist Hymnal* (Nashville: The United Methodist Publishing House, 1989), trans. sts. 2 and 4.

[2] John 3:16, NIV, emphasis mine: "For God so loved the *world* that he gave his one and only Son..."

Day Three

THE TRAGEDY OF DELAY

The harvest is past, the summer has ended, and we are not saved.

—Jeremiah 8:20 NIV

I ONCE HEARD A STORY TOLD ABOUT SATAN GIVING HIS FINAL INSTRUCtions to his three newest recruits before they were sent to the earth to deceive the people. Satan asks his first minion, "What is the first thing you will tell the people on earth?"

The first minion thinks for a minute and says, "I will tell them there is no Heaven." Satan responds and says, "That will not work. Many people already believe there is a Heaven."

Satan turns to his next minion and asks, "What is the first thing you will tell the people on earth?" This second minion also ponders this question for a minute and says, "I will tell them there is no hell." Satan, disappointed, says, "That will also not work, as many people, too, believe there is a hell."

Satan, frustrated, turns to his third minion and asks, "What is the first thing you will tell the people on earth?" Without any hesitation or thought, he responds, "I will tell them there is no hurry." Satan, the master of deception, responds, "You are exactly correct." He instructs his three new recruits to leave now to spread the deceptive lie and tell everyone, "There is no hurry."

I titled this Day Three devotion "The Tragedy of Delay" for one simple but paramount reason. Any amount of delay in making that commitment to Jesus is deadly. There are many reasons people do not accept Jesus as Lord and Savior now but choose to wait. I realize there are people out there who are hard of heart and so blind they refuse to accept Jesus. Those who are so narrow-minded that if they cannot see or cannot touch something, they shut the door on believing. Too, there are those who refuse to believe that they are sinful in nature and, therefore, believe they have no need for a savior.

I know of folks who are so turned off by "religion" and problems in the Church that their default reaction to Jesus is simply no. Another reason given a lot is the question, "Why would such a loving god (as you Christians profess) allow bad things to happen to good people?" But I truly believe that a primary reason, maybe not the main one but pretty close, is delay and procrastination.

Let me flesh this out some. Many of us, by nature, put things off.

"I will get to it tomorrow."

"The time is just not right today."

"Man, I have all these other things that are taking priority and need my attention now."

I will have to admit that I suffer from this procrastination syndrome. For a simple example, I have a closet that needs cleaning out, and I walk in it every day and say to myself every day, "I need to

THE TRAGEDY OF DELAY

clean this out. What a mess." Well, it still needs cleaning out as I write this devotional. Another personal example of delay and procrastination is my daughter, Kat.[1] When she was in high school and even in undergraduate and graduate school at the University of South Carolina, she would, at times, wait until the last minute to complete that project or study for that exam. And boy, her stress level was on the high side of the anxiety meter. Even though she did very well each time, she still put herself through a lot of anxiety. By the way, she was Phi Beta Kappa in college.

We must understand this. Any delay in accepting Jesus has two sides. Here is what I mean. Not only is a delay in our personal commitment to Christ deadly, but any delay in bringing others, especially our children, to Christ is equally as deadly.

One absolute truth is that everyone is going to die. The second absolute truth is that no one knows the day and time of our respective deaths except our Father in Heaven. The third absolute truth is that we don't get a second chance after we die. The fourth absolute truth is that death is blackness, defeat, and despair. The fifth absolute truth is that Heaven is glorious, full of joy, and alive. Why risk the chance of not spending eternity with Jesus and our loved ones simply because it is not a convenient time to make a commitment? Why allow delay and procrastination to win out over the simple choice of accepting Jesus as Lord and Savior in your life? The choice for each of us is to choose not to be lost but to be found in the arms of a loving Jesus one day.

But we cannot stop here! We cannot allow delay to prevent us from sharing the Gospel with others, especially our loved ones. I read a story about a funeral service being held for a little girl who died in a tragic accident. It was conducted by a visiting pastor who did not know the family or the community. He asked the parents, "Was she saved?" The parents replied, "We do not know. We intended to talk with her, but we put it off, and the days passed."

The pastor went to the little girl's Sunday School teacher and asked the same question: "Was she saved?" The teacher replied that she did not know. She had meant to talk with the little girl but did not.

The pastor went to the Sunday School superintendent and asked the same question, and the superintendent gave the same response as the parents and Sunday School teacher did.[2]

Can you think of a more terrible and tragic situation than that? We have a responsibility to others and to our children to take the time to tell them about Jesus. No one would wish eternity outside of Heaven on our worst enemies, much less our people who we love and are close to.

So here is the plan. We must remove from our thoughts that we are too busy. That we will get to it one day, but not now. That the time is just not right. That we have more important things to do. Throw these ideas away as far as you can. Now, if you have not made the commitment, do so now. Please accept the fact that you are a sinner and are in need of a Savior. Then, recognize Jesus as your Savior, knowing that He died on the cross for the forgiveness of your sins and that He came alive three days later, so eternal salvation is within your reach.

Once you do that, do not stop there! Please do not stop! Go to someone you know and explain this commitment to them and encourage them to accept it now. Then go to your child. Tell them God loves them so much that Jesus sacrificed His life for them and that He defeated death three days later so they could spend all eternity in Heaven.

Accept this challenge. The alternative is not good. Remember, delays create death! Delays create catastrophe! Delays cause tragedy! Time is of the essence!

Thought: What are some reasons why you have delayed in reaching out to someone and talking with them about Christ?

Let us pray: Lord, You have made it clear in scripture that You are patient and that You want everyone, yes everyone, to be saved. Please never allow anyone to delay in coming to Christ or delay in bringing someone to Christ.

THE TRAGEDY OF DELAY

Provide the realization that accepting Jesus as Lord and Savior is the most important decision anyone can ever make. Amen.

---

[1] I got her permission to use this example so long as, according to her, I do not leave her under the "bus," but pull her out.

[2] Story taken from the W.A. Criswell Library, July 20, 2024. Let me address an issue that you may be thinking about. Some believe, as I do, that Jesus has a special plan for children for eternal purposes, and some believe the contrary. Of course, we do not know what age would be involved in this special plan. Therefore, I tell this story to show why it is so important to tell our children about Jesus at any age.

Day Four

THE INCARNATION OF JESUS

Who, being in very nature God, did not consider equality with God something to be used to his own advantage; rather, he made himself nothing by taking the very nature of a servant, being made in human likeness, and being found in appearance as a man, he humbled himself by becoming obedient to death—even death on a cross!

—Philippians 2:6–8 NIV

I HAVE ALWAYS BEEN FASCINATED WITH JESUS BEING FULLY HUMAN along with being fully divine. Yes, He was both, and it was essential that He be both to accomplish the purposes and goals of God. But my focus of this devotional will be on Jesus' complete humanity during the time He lived on this earth. This idea that He would come to this earth and live and breathe just like you and me is so intriguing. He was incarnate from the Holy Spirit and the Virgin Mary and was made man. His birth was just like your birth and my birth, and He was fully clothed in flesh just like us as well.

So, let's take a look at why it was necessary for the divine Jesus to come to this earth as a human, and then we will take a look at some specific examples of Jesus' humanity and why it is important to us today.

First, I believe God determined that the best way for Jesus to relate to humans in the fullest was to be another human being. Is that not so true in our relationships with others? Similarity and familiarity always foster good and strong relationships. We are always attracted to those like us.

Secondly, Jesus right now intercedes for us in Heaven. (See Romans 8:34.) Knowing what it is like to be a human and experiencing all the emotions, wants, desires, and, yes, temptations only puts Jesus in a better position to help us in times of need.

Thirdly and lastly and probably most importantly, a divine Jesus could not experience the agony, the sorrow, and the overwhelming feeling as the human Jesus did in the Garden of Gethsemane and on the cross. A divine Jesus, in the garden, would not have sweated blood, as recorded in the Gospel of Luke (Luke 22), pleading with the Father to take the cup from Him. A divine Jesus, on the barbaric cross, could not have been the one to die the horrendous death for the forgiveness of our sins. No, it had to be a human Jesus to take this mission on. This mission to die for us and come alive for us becomes more real and more amazing, illustrating just how much God loves us.

Now, let's take a look at some specific examples of Jesus being as human as human can be. Several years ago, I went through the four Gospels and counted how many times He did something that you and I would do or have done many times in the past. Now, I am sure I missed some, but I counted 14 times in Matthew, 22 in Mark, 27 in Luke, and 20 times in John. Here we go with a few examples:

Jesus Gave Thanks: Matthew 26:26-27

Jesus gave thanks at the Last Supper. Knowing what was awaiting Him with the impending death on the cross, Jesus was still thankful to His God. We too should always give thanks to our Father in heaven regardless of the circumstances. The apostle Paul tells us to "give thanks in all circumstances."[1] We should always follow Jesus' lead.

Jesus Fell to the Ground and Prayed: Mark 14:35

There is absolutely no question that Jesus prayed a lot. This one human activity is mentioned more in the four Gospels than anything else. Jesus was always going off somewhere private to pray. We should pray daily and constantly throughout the day. Prayers of gratitude, prayers for forgiveness, prayers of intercession, and prayers of praise and worship should always be a regular part of our lives. Having that daily conversation with our Father in Heaven is crucial to everyone's faith journey. Thank Him, praise Him—you will be glad you did.

Jesus Was Full of the Holy Spirit: Luke 4:1

This account of Jesus in the Gospel of Luke was when He, full of the Holy Spirit, was led into the wilderness where He spent forty days and then was tempted by Satan. I am confident that the Holy Spirit got the human Jesus through this ordeal without succumbing to the wiles of the devil. When someone comes to faith and believes in Jesus and what He has done for us, God sends His Holy Spirit to live within that person. We have the power of the Holy Spirit to guide and direct us, to protect us, and to lead us through everything that life throws at us. Jesus relied on the Holy Spirit! We should too!

Jesus Wept: John 11:35

Jesus showed His compassionate side at the death of His dear friend, Lazarus. Jesus, during His three years of His ministry on this earth, simply displayed a big heart. He showed compassion for so many people when He healed them from illness, disease, and even death. He brought Lazarus back to life from death soon after He shed those tears. Jesus continues to show that He still has a big heart and that He will cry along with us when the hurt, the pain, and the trauma are real. We should go to Jesus daily. He knows our needs, and He will hold us in His arms and cry with us and bring us to safety.

Thought: Do you ever think about Jesus being both totally divine and totally human? What part of His human side can you relate to the best?

Let us pray: Jesus, my friend and Savior! I know that Your plan with God would not have worked if You had not been fully human when You came to this earth. You experienced many of the things I experience today, and how wonderful it is that You can intercede for me, knowing exactly what I am going through. How wonderful it is! Amen.

---

[1] 1 Thessalonians 5:18a NIV

Day Five

PRAISE TO GOD

For what you have done I will always praise you in the presence of your faithful people. And I will hope in your name, for your name is good.

—Psalm 52:9 NIV

W<small>E ALL LIKE TO BE PRAISED. </small>T<small>HAT IS SIMPLY HUMAN NATURE. </small>P<small>RAISE</small> when we are young and when we are old and any time in between. Praise provides that positive reinforcement to do as good or even better next time in that same endeavor. It boosts self-confidence and self-esteem. I know when my children, Michael and Kat, were growing up, praise was a constant in our household by my wife, Gayle, and me. Whether it was in sports, academics, or just being all-around great kids, we always praised our kids. While the praise was certainly good for our children, that praise was good for Gayle and me as well. When we saw those smiles on their faces and that sense of pride (good pride), that kinda' glow from their demeanor, then, oh man, our hearts were warmed because we knew they felt good, which we always wanted for our kids. It simply brought us joy and brought us closer to our children.

Please allow me to share a very recent example where praise was showered on our grandson, Ford.[1] A day before writing this devotional was Ford's first day at 5K school. Ford shed a few tears but not many. He was a real trooper. Other students who were dropped off had a harder time. There was one boy who was hysterical when his mom left, and Ford went over to the boy and hugged him to console him. We have the most precious picture of that. And boy, did Gayle and I and his parents, Michael and Mandy, load him up with praise. So proud of him.

Now, let's turn our attention to the focus of this devotional—praising God. I want to begin with a significant event in my family that has kept praise to God at the center of our lives. On August 6, 2023, our son, Michael, while up in a bucket truck 20 feet in the air, working for the City of Laurens Commission of Public Works, fell out of the bucket to the ground. A storm had passed through on a Sunday afternoon, and Michael's crew was called out to fix the damage caused by the storm. He was dealing with a tree that was dangerously close to a power line. The next thing he remembers, he was out of the bucket and the safety harness, falling through tree limbs to the ground. My friends, by the grace of God, Michael survived. Praise God! He broke his back in three places, his tailbone, and also his sternum. He spent a week in intensive care and two weeks in an in-patient facility for rehabilitation. He continues to go twice a week for outpatient physical therapy. I tell you this story because we praise God every day for saving our son. It was by the hand of God, and His hand alone, that Michael survived the fall.

There are two things I want you to remember from this devotional. First, praising God will bring us much joy and bring us closer to our Heavenly Father as with our children. Secondly, every time we give thanks to God, we should always follow it with praise. He

PRAISE TO GOD

is the source of everything and certainly what we have give Him thanks for. He created this world we live in. He brought us Jesus, who died for the forgiveness of our many sins. He brought Jesus back to life so that we can have an eternal home in Heaven. He showers us with grace upon grace. God is so worthy of our praise.

So here is what I am asking of my readers. After you have read this devotional and maybe studied on it for a few minutes, close the book and think of one thing in your life that you can praise God for. Start off with thanksgiving and follow it up with praise. Praise can be through prayer, song, scripture reading, or deciding on a change in lifestyle that evidences an obedience to God. Whatever it is, praise Him, praise Him, praise Him.

Thank You, God, and praise be to You!

Thought: What in your life are you thankful for? In which areas of your life can you give God all praise and honor? What does that look like?

Let us pray: Dear Heavenly and gracious Lord, You are an awesome God who deserves all praise and honor. Give me a grateful heart and never let a day go by where I do not praise You and praise Your holy name. Amen.

---

[1] I have talked about Ford in my previous two books and said that he is a great kid. I want you to know that he is still a great kid.

Day Six

MISSION POSSIBLE

But you, dear friends, by building yourselves up in your most holy faith and praying in the Holy Spirit, keep yourselves in God's love as you wait for the mercy of our Lord Jesus Christ to bring you to eternal life. Be merciful to those who doubt; save others by snatching them from the fire; to others show mercy, mixed with fear—hating even the clothing stained by corrupted flesh.

—Jude 1:20–23 NIV

BACK IN THE 60S AND 70S, THERE WAS A TELEVISION SHOW CALLED *Mission Impossible,* which preceded the highly successful *Mission Impossible* movies with Tom Cruise. The television show would always begin with a reel-to-reel tape recorder, and the recording would go like this: "Good morning." Then the voice would explain the national security problem and then say, "Your mission, should you decide to accept it…" and the voice would explain the assignment. Then the voice would conclude, "If you get caught or killed, the secretary will disavow any knowledge of you. This tape will self-destruct in five seconds." Next, you would see smoke coming out of this tape recorder.[1]

The key phrase in the opening segment of this television show is "Your mission, should you decide to accept it…" Well, we have a mission, and if we've truly made Jesus the Lord of our lives, then we do not have the option of deciding whether or not to accept it. Let's look at two New Testament examples where Jesus' commands are very clear.

The first example is known as Jesus' Great Commission.

> Therefore go and make disciples of all nations, baptizing them in the name of the Father and of the Son and of the Holy Spirit, and teaching them to obey everything I have commanded you. And surely I am with you always, to the very end of the age. (Matt. 28:19–20 NIV)

The second example is Jesus' last instruction before He was taken up to Heaven.

> But you will receive power when the Holy Spirit comes on you; and you will be my witnesses in Jerusalem, and in all Judea and Samaria and to the ends of the earth. (Acts 1:8 NIV)

While the above two examples are when Jesus was instructing His disciples, these instructions are for us as well.

Jesus isn't the only person in scripture who sets a mission before believers. Let's look at the great apostle Paul and what he says we are to do:

How, then, can they call on the one they have not believed in? And how can they believe in the one of whom they have not heard? And how can they hear without someone preaching to them? And how can anyone preach unless they are sent? As it is written: "How beautiful are the feet of those who bring good news!" (Rom. 10:14–15 NIV)

Whatever happens, conduct yourselves in a manner worthy of the gospel of Christ. Then, whether I come and see you or only hear about you in my absence, I will know that you stand firm in the one Spirit, striving together as one for the faith of the Gospel. (Phil. 1:27 NIV)

And then to piggyback on what our Lord Jesus and Paul told us, we need to take one more step and look at what the disciple John says:

If anyone has material possessions and sees a brother or sister in need but has no pity on them, how can the love of God be in that person?" (1 John 3:17 NIV).]

We have to be mindful of the fact that these scriptural instructions are not optional, nor do they give us any wiggle room. We have been commanded to be on a mission for God. Based on these verses, what is our mission? What is the reel-to-reel tape recorder telling us?

First, we are to be strong in our faith. We cannot do anything for God if we do not have a solid foundation in our faith. How in the world can we promote the Kingdom if we are not rock solid in our beliefs? We have a mission-type statement at my church, and it is BOLD—Becoming Obedient Loving Disciples (of Jesus Christ). Simply stated, we must first be a strong disciple of Jesus before we can do anything else.

Secondly, we are to witness for Jesus and make as many disciples as we can for the Kingdom. John Piper, in his book *The Only Way to God*, says, "Christians are called arrogant and hateful because of our belief that Jesus is the only way of salvation. Many shrink back from affirming the global necessity of knowing and believing in Jesus." We cannot be shy, nor a coward, in spreading the Good News. We must be bold!

Lastly, we must show love and compassion for others. Show the heart of the Father that our Lord and Savior Jesus Christ showed when He was on this earth. Take care of the needy. Take care of those less fortunate. Use the resources God has given us. We should never look the other way.

The great thing is that God will never disavow us as the tape recording says. No, He is with us every step of the way. Jesus promised us this in the earlier passage from Matthew. That is what brings peace, hope, and comfort to believers.

Our mission is to make possible what appears to be impossible. Show love to those who appear to be unlovable. Grant mercy to those who maybe do not deserve mercy. Spread the good news of the Gospel. Bring as many to Christ as we can. Take care of those who are needy. Becoming rock solid in our faith, being a witness for Jesus, and showing compassion may all feel impossible sometimes. We can, however, make possible what appears to be impossible. The mission is possible! The mission is accepted!

Thought: Are you willing to accept this mission? What is one thing you can do to fulfill part of the mission right now for God?

Let us pray: Dear Lord, Your Spirit lives within every believer. Help me to seek Your most Holy Spirit's guidance and direction as I take on Your mission to build up Your Kingdom here on earth and to make as many people disciples of Christ. Keep me strong and focused. Amen.

---

[1] The *Mission Impossible* movies with Tom Cruise would have a similar opening using high-tech digital equipment. I like the old reel-to-reel recorder.

Day Seven

GIVING UP CONTROL

Trust in the Lord with all your heart and lean not on your own understanding; in all your ways submit to him, and he will make your paths straight.

—Proverbs 3:5–6 NIV

By nature, I am one who likes to be in control of whatever situation I am in. In light of that, one of the hardest things I have ever had to do is teach Michael and Kat how to drive. Now let me say right at the outset, both were very good drivers growing up and are also currently. Back in the early days of their driving, when they were behind the wheel and had complete control of the gas pedal and brake, being in the passenger seat—completely at the mercy of a fifteen-year-old—it was a bad feeling.[1]

No, the more I think of it, it was worse than a bad feeling. I received no parental training in undergoing this task of teaching my kids to drive. No warning whatsoever. Where was the manual for this? I was riding in several thousand pounds of machinery that I had no control over, all the while sweating, not breathing, gripping the armrest of the passenger door, my right foot pounding the floorboard, looking for that passenger-side brake. Thanks, GM, for not installing that absolutely necessary accessory! And top it all off, each one of my kids would look over at me while I was convulsing and turning green, and they would assure me with this statement: "Dad, don't worry. I have got this!" But I survived! Kind of![2]

Relinquishing control to God! Now that is another control area that we all struggle with. I do a lot better with this now than I did before I was saved, but admittedly, I still struggle with it at times. Why is it that we, especially us men, have such a hard time giving up that desire to influence a situation with an unhealthy amount of control? To handle whatever it is that comes our way? Why is it so difficult to exercise some self-restraint? Why is it so hard to admit we cannot handle a predicament we are in and simply say, "God, please take over?"

I believe that if we are really honest with ourselves, giving up control boils down to these three things:

1. *Lack of Trust:* We do not always trust that God is all-knowing and all-powerful. We question whether or not He is up to the task or if He even cares about the situation we find ourselves in. Probably the main doubt we have is that God will not act as soon as we believe He needs to. This dilemma we are in needs immediate action, and God is not going to act as soon as we believe that He needs to. We simply do not practice that trust in our Heavenly Father.

2. *Our Selfish Nature:* We are, by nature, selfish creatures. Self gets in the way more times than we care to admit. If we would remove ourselves from the equation and give it to God, outcomes would be far better. You see, we want to go in the direction that is more pleasant, more pleasing, and satisfying to our wants and desires. Make me happy, and all is well.

GIVING UP CONTROL

3. Our False Sense of Ability: We lack humility, and therefore, we believe we are equipped with all of the essentials to meet that challenge, to take that path. We so oftentimes think that we are better suited than God to make the decisions in whatever we encounter. We can be so self-centered that we fail to fully grasp the idea that the God of our universe, who created everything and everyone, is able to handle this one issue that this one human is confronted with.

So, what is the cure for our need to control? What is the answer that will allow us to loosen the grip on life's steering wheel and give everything up to God? These are some ideas, and it all begins with prayer:

Pray for Humility: We need to have a modest assessment of our self-worth and our abilities mixed in with a true realization that we are sinful creatures.

Pray for Clarity: We need to have a clear mindset that God has infinite abilities and wisdom to handle any situation we lay at His feet. There is absolutely nothing He cannot do.

Pray for Self-Forgetting: We need to always put our selfish motives and desires way in the back seat of our lives and never allow them to have influence when situations creep in or come full throttle into our lives.

Pray for Confidence: We need to have that confident trust in our Lord, knowing, without question, that He is the Creator and Sustainer of all life, all that there is, and all that there will be. If He can bring people back to life from the dead, which He certainly can and has done, He can handle any and all problems that we have. Just remember, God told the prophet Jeremiah, "I am the Lord, the God of all mankind. Is anything too hard for me?"[3]

Maybe you are facing a career change and do not know what to do. Give it to God. Maybe you are facing a health problem and do not know what treatment option is best. Give it to God. Maybe you have a family member who is going through a crisis and seeks your advice, and you do not know what to do. Give it to God.

So, are we going to do what the lyrics say in Carrie Underwood's famous song "Jesus Take the Wheel"?[4] "Take it from my hands 'cause I can't do this on my own." Are we going to decide it is time to give to God our life's steering wheel? There is not a better time than now!

Thought: Think of times when you have and have not given up control to God. Compare the outcomes of both.

Let us pray: Dear Almighty God, never let a minute go by that I do not look to You for strength, guidance, and direction. Help me to always lay any problem I have at Your feet, knowing You will take control and the outcome will always be perfect and true. Amen.

---

[1] I am sure many of you can relate to this ordeal!

[2] As I said, both are very good drivers! No traffic tickets or accidents that were their fault—at least, not that I am of .

[3] Jeremiah 32:27 NIV

[4] *Some Hearts*, released in 2005. Song written by Hillery Lindsey, Brett James, Gordie Sampson.

Day Eight

SATAN'S IMPOSTOR

Now for some time a man named Simon had practiced sorcery in the city and amazed all the people of Samaria. He boasted that he was someone great, and all the people, both high and low, gave him their attention and exclaimed, "This man is rightly called the Great Power of God." They followed him because he had amazed them for a long time with his sorcery. But when they believed Philip as he proclaimed the good news of the kingdom of God and the name of Jesus Christ, they were baptized, both men and women. Simon himself believed and was baptized. And he followed Philip everywhere, astonished by the great signs and miracles he saw. When the apostles in Jerusalem heard that Samaria had accepted the word of God, they sent Peter and John to Samaria. When they arrived, they prayed for the new believers there that they might receive the Holy Spirit, because the Holy Spirit had not yet come on any of them; they had simply been baptized in the name of the Lord Jesus. Then Peter and John placed their hands on them, and they received the Holy Spirit. When Simon saw that the Spirit was given at the laying on of the apostles' hands, he offered them money and said, "Give me also this ability so that everyone on whom I lay my hands may receive the Holy Spirit." Peter answered: "May your money perish with you, because you thought you could buy the gift of God with money! You have no part or share in this ministry, because your heart is not right before God. Repent of this wickedness and pray to the Lord in the hope that he may forgive you for having such a thought in your heart. For I see that you are full of bitterness and captive to sin." Then Simon answered, "Pray to the Lord for me so that nothing you have said may happen to me." After they had further proclaimed the word of the Lord and testified about Jesus, Peter and John returned to Jerusalem, preaching the gospel in many Samaritan villages.

—Acts 8:9–25 NIV

THE 2002 MOVIE *CATCH ME IF YOU CAN*,[1] STARRING LEONARDO DiCaprio, is a real-life story[2] about a man named Frank Abagnale.[3] He posed as a doctor, a lawyer, and a co-pilot of a major airline without possessing any of the requisite training, education, and degrees. He was a master of deception. A fraud, a counterfeit, an impostor.

What is Satan's Imposter? Let's explore that phrase I coined by studying the story of Simon the Sorcerer. This story is one of my favorite stories in the Bible that is filled with so much theology, meaning, and truth. Of course, part of the mix is our good ol' friend Peter of the twelve-disciples fame who lays some much-deserved "smackdown" on Simon. I want to highlight this story from the Book of Acts and then tie it into today's Satan and unfortunately you and me.

Right off the bat, we learn that Simon was a part of Satan's team. He was a sorcerer. A master at witchcraft, voodoo, and magic which amazed everyone. Satan, being the expert deceiver, helped Simon deceive the people as they thought Simon had the "power of God." So then Philip, another disciple of Jesus, came on the scene and began preaching and baptizing the folks in that region. So Simon thought he wanted to get in on some of this action, so he started following Philip, and in verse 13, it says, "Simon himself believed and was baptized." Really? Maybe Simon was doing some deceitful work on himself.

Anyways, in came the "heavyweights from Jerusalem," Peter and John, to check things out. Peter and John came to the conclusion that the Samaritans were coming to faith but were still missing something, and that was the Holy Spirit. So, Peter and John laid hands on the people, and they received the Holy Spirit. Simon saw all of this and, I am sure, said to himself, "Yeah, I need this Holy Spirit to be in my bag of tricks!" So what did Simon do? Can you believe this? He offered money to Peter and John to be able to lay hands on people so that they could receive the Holy Spirit. See, Simon was still in the performance mode, intent on glorifying himself and not God.

This is where our beloved Peter laid the smackdown on Simon. Peter said in verse 20, "May your money perish with you." In other words, "Simon, keep your filthy money!" Peter did not stop there. He told Simon he better pray to God and repent of his sin. Otherwise, no forgiveness for you. Then, with one last nail in the coffin that showed his true colors, Simon asked Peter to pray in his place. Now, nothing wrong with asking the "Great Rock of the Church," Peter, to pray for you, but certainly not in the heart posture Simon had. He had no intention of becoming a true believer. Simon had no intention of having the Holy Spirit fill his total being. No, Simon, while having Satan be a cheerleader for him on the sidelines, was only interested in himself. Simply stated, Simon was truly Satan's Impostor.

So, how can we avoid being called Satan's Impostor? How can we learn not to allow Satan to cause us to act all pious and genuine but with a heart not fully invested in the Lord? The absolute starting point is believing without hesitation that Satan is real and alive and active every single day. There is a real spiritual battle going on in the lives of Christians, and we have to be ready for the evil one. If Satan took on Jesus in the wilderness,[4] don't you think he will not hesitate to take on you and me? So, what can we learn from Simon the Sorcerer? Here are some things to consider:

1. Never take the credit. Always give credit where credit is due—our Father in Heaven.

2. Never get wrapped up in the glitz and glam of religion. In another words, when at church or some other religious venue, focus your mind and heart on worship of our Lord and do not get side-tracked with the great choirs or contemporary bands, the magnificent church buildings and stain-glass windows, or the "Billy Graham" sermons. Keep it real!

3. Make sure your faith is real and not bogus. Make sure your faith is built on a strong relationship with God, a true and sincere realization and appreciation that Jesus went to the cross for only this reason—for the forgiveness of our sins—and that God brought Jesus back to life so that we can have eternal life with Him.

4. Always treat the Holy Spirit as a gift from God.

5. Truly realize that as an extension of Jesus's death on the cross is our confession and repentance of our sins.

6. Always act in the same way you talk. In other words, never talk about Jesus and then act as if He does not exist.

7. Do not be deceitful as Simon was. Never act as if your relationship with the Lord is better than it really is.

I have said this many times. When we are standing before Jesus, we do not want Him to say, "Your faith has not been real. You have been a fake!" Oh no, that would be terrible. We want to hear the

SATAN'S IMPOSTOR

words, "Come in, my good and faithful servant"! Yes, those words will be sweet music to my ears and yours!

Thought: Think of a time when you have acted as an impostor and not a true follower of Christ. Were you able to avoid it the next time?

Let us pray: Lord, keep my thoughts pure, my heart real, and my actions sincere. Help me to keep my faith in You strong, and in all that I do, I do it for Your honor and glory. Amen.

---

[1] Produced and directed by Steven Spielberg. Screenplay by Jeff Nathanson. Distributed by Dreamworks Pictures.

[2] Many dispute the truth and accuracy of this story.

[3] He wrote a book by the same name as the movie, which the movie is based on.

[4] See Luke 4:1–13. A great story about temptation and the power of the Holy Spirit.

Day Nine

RESERVATION IN HEAVEN

Do not let your hearts be troubled. You believe in God; believe also in me. My Father's house has many rooms; if that were not so, would I have told you that I am going there to prepare a place for you? And if I go and prepare a place for you, I will come back and take you to be with me that you also may be where I am. You know the way to the place where I am going.

—John 14:1–4 NIV

I DO NOT KNOW ABOUT YOU, BUT I FIND MAKING RESERVATIONS AT A hotel or a restaurant troubling. Let me explain why. It seems now that if you need to make a reservation at a hotel, you cannot call the individual hotel. Oh, no! That is too easy. You have to call a central number to make the reservation. No telling where this person on the other end of the line is located, but you know for sure they are not close—maybe not in this country. Anyways, I was working out of town several years ago in a city in South Carolina known as Moncks Corner.[1] Needless to say, it took longer than expected to nail down a reservation at the central reservation station.

Also, what about restaurants? Nowadays, you cannot simply pick up the phone and call the restaurant. No, you have to have an app on your phone for the restaurant to make it. Gayle's birthday is June 7, so we decided to go to a fancy restaurant for dinner. I went to the website for the restaurant and saw that, from all indications, reservations could be made there. I put in all the necessary information and thought we were good to go. Arriving at the restaurant, I gave the girl at the front my name and time of the reservation, fully expecting the girl to say, "Please come this way, Mr. Hocker," and anticipating a great meal at this restaurant. Instead, I heard the girl say, "I am sorry, Mr. Hocker. We do not show you down for a 7:30 reservation." It turns out I needed an app for this restaurant to make a reservation. Dang website did not tell me this. Oh well. However, we were able to go to another fine restaurant, so everything did work out.

The great thing about our passage from the Gospel of John is that we do not have to call some central number or have an app on our phone in order to make reservations in Heaven. No, no, no! Our reservations have already been made. They were made the very moment we accepted Jesus Christ as our Lord and Savior. Let me share with you something I read recently, and it goes like this:

> When we give our lives fully to Jesus Christ, we begin the journey to becoming the person He created us to be. We are God's masterpiece, created anew in Christ Jesus for good works which He has already prepared for us. He is our true Father and *our real home* is with Him, now and forever. (emphasis mine)[2]

RESERVATION IN HEAVEN

Yes, Heaven is our real home where believers will spend all of eternity with the Father and Jesus. Jesus has promised us this, and He never goes back on His promises.

Not only has Jesus promised us that there is a Heaven and it does exist, but He has also promised us that there will be plenty of rooms for many people. This tells me that its size is infinite without boundaries. It will hold a lot of people. Past, current, and future believers will be there, and God is counting on more believers to accept His offer of hope and salvation. We are reminded that God is a patient God, not wanting anyone to perish.[3] In other words, God wants everyone to be saved and reside eternally with Him in Heaven. Sadly, though, He knows that will not be the case.

Jesus also promises us that He personally is getting our future home ready for us. It is like the clean linens and towels are being put on the hotel bed and in the hotel bathroom before check-in. Or the table is being set with the restaurant's finest china and silver. What a place Heaven will be!

Finally, Jesus promises us He Himself will take us to Heaven—our personal chauffeur escorting us to our real home, and what a trip that will be!

I take Jesus' promises at His word. I do not doubt nor question what He tells us. I simply take His promise of Heaven as my confirmation number that my reservation is secure. There is no better hope than that!

Thought: When did you have Jesus make your reservation in Heaven? How does knowing your place is secure make you feel?

Let us pray: Dear Wonderful Jesus, thank You for Your promise of Heaven and Your assurance that Heaven is real. Thank You that You are getting it ready for me and that You will personally bring me home. Amen.

[1] I am sure glad I did not have to make the reservations for Denmark, South Carolina. Yes, it is a real city.

[2] Francine Rivers, published 2/23/23. Internet Daily Bible Living. *Five Subtle Ways.*

[3] See 2 Peter 3:9 NIV.

Day Ten

PERFECTION

Not that I have already obtained all this, or have already arrived at my goal, but I press on to take hold of that for which Christ Jesus took hold of me.

—Philippians 3:12 NIV

If we claim to be without sin, we deceive ourselves and the truth is not in us.

—1 John 1:8 NIV

Without a doubt, there has only been one person—past, present, or future—who walked on the face of this earth that we can say was perfect, and that is Jesus. Why was He perfect? Because He was without sin. Even though He was totally human, He was totally divine, and that divine nature kept Him perfect, sinless, and without blemish of any kind.

On the other hand, every other person—past, present, or future—who has walked or will walk on the face of this earth is on the complete opposite end of the spectrum and is imperfect and full of sin. Making mistakes, taking the wrong turns, forming bad decisions, and in some instances not trying to achieve goals or successful endeavors. These are behaviors that we should try to avoid.

However, striving for perfection has taken a bad rap in our culture and society. I came across a quote once that said, "Perfectionism is the voice of the oppressor, the enemy of the people. It will keep you insane your whole life." Whoa! Well, maybe that is true for secular things in this world. But what about perfection as in striving to be more Christ-like? Jesus Himself said, "Be perfect, therefore, as your heavenly Father is perfect."[1] Jesus wants us, all of us, to simply be more like Him. That is definitely a good thing, right?

In the above passage in Philippians, Paul is essentially telling us to press on towards what Christ has shown us. That was Paul's goal and should also be our goal. Then, going further, Peter tells us, "To this you were called, because Christ suffered for you, leaving you an example, that you should follow in his steps. He committed no sin, and no deceit was found in his mouth."[2] Exactly. Follow in Jesus' steps, which means to be more like Him. So, if Jesus, Paul, and Peter are telling us to be more like Jesus, meaning striving towards perfection, then by golly, that is what we should do.

Now we know that we will never get there, but we should always rely on the power of the Holy Spirit and the blood of Jesus to try and get there as far as we can. So how do we strive towards perfection? Let me start off by saying that believing you are a good person really is not what I am talking about here. Let me explain. I am a huge Denzel Washington[3] fan. In one of his recent movies, his character was injured, and a police officer took him to the local doctor's house for treatment. The doctor asked him, "Did I save a good man or a bad man?" Denzel's character responded, "I do not know."

PERFECTION

Later in the movie, when recovery was about completed, the doctor asked him if he remembered the question that he had been asked. Denzel's character said he did, and the doctor replied, "Only a good man would have answered the question in the way that you did."

I think what this film clip is telling us is that if you do not know if you are really a good person or bad person, then you are recognizing there is a good chance that not only are you in a big need for a savior, you have got some work to do to become more like Jesus. If you answered, "I am a good man," then maybe you are fooling yourself into believing that there is no need for a savior and that "being good" is enough. My friends, we have work to do! So, what are some things we can "work" on in our efforts to sincerely and maturely strive to be more like Jesus?

Compassion: What a big heart Jesus had! He never turned down an opportunity to heal someone, to feed thousands at a time, or to teach simple truths that certain people needed to hear. We must show compassion for others in need whether it is working in the local food bank, writing a donation check to ministries that provide help to those experiencing disasters, visiting shut-ins members in your church, or refusing to pass by that person holding up a sign that says, "Need Food." Whatever it is, allow your compassionate heart to govern your actions.

Love: I know some people are hard to love, but they need to be loved anyway. Look at Jesus. Who did He hang out with? Yep, those unlovables, the outcasts, the tax collectors, those that society did not care much for. I am not suggesting that we should all turn into a flower child of the 1960s,[4]—wearing flowers, making peace signs, and talking about "groovy love." No, what I am suggesting is that we all recognize that everyone is a creature of God with needs and weaknesses. Everyone is sinful, and it is only by God's grace that forgiveness saves the day. Just extend some grace. It will do you good.

Justice: We need to stand up for what is right and true. In today's culture, everyone believes in their own truth. You have your own truth, and I have mine. We say, "Don't tell me what my truth should be, and I will not tell you what yours should be." How many times did Jesus speak the truth? How many times did Jesus offend those pesky Pharisees who were the righteous spiritual leaders of the day? He never backed down, especially when He called them hypocrites. In all of His parables, He always made a point that was right and true. We should do the same thing. We should never hesitate to approach a situation that is wrong, unjust, or contrary to God's will. We should make the truth be known. There may be a cost to taking this risk. There sure was a cost to Jesus. But being just is always worth the cost.

Being more like Jesus is our major task at hand as we are commanded to do. This devotional provides a start on our road to perfection.

Thought: Is it important to you to be more like Jesus? What are some practical things you can do to be more like Jesus?

Let us pray: Dear Jesus, instill in me that burning desire to be more like You in all that I do and say. Give me that heart of compassion and love. Amen.

---

[1] Matthew 5:48 NIV

[2] 1 Peter 2:22 NIV

[3] I just learned that he recently became an ordained minister. I like the guy even more!

[4] In 1967, their big movement was in San Francisco labeled by the media as the "Summer of Love."

Day Eleven

DO THE RIGHT THING

Shadrach, Meshach, and Abednego replied to him, "King Nebuchadnezzar, we do not need to defend ourselves before you in this matter. If we are thrown into the blazing furnace, the God we serve is able to deliver us from it, and he will deliver us from Your Majesty's hand. But even if he does not, we want you to know, Your Majesty, that we will not serve your gods or worship the image of gold you have set up."

Daniel 3:16–18 NIV

THE BOOK OF DANIEL IN THE OLD TESTAMENT STARTS OFF WITH Nebuchadnezzar, king of Babylon, besieging the city of Jerusalem in Judah and taking as captives fit young men who could be trained to enter into the king's service. Four of these young men were Daniel and his three friends, Hananiah, Mishael, and Azariah. The king changed their names, and Daniel's three friends became Shadrach, Meshach, and Abednego, the stars of today's passage.

The king made a large golden image that he required everyone to bow down to and worship at designated times during the day. These courageous young men refused, and Daniel's three friends were summoned by the king. They stood up to the king, knowing full well what was going to happen. (See today's passage). The king was furious, and as verse 19 says, "He ordered the furnace heated seven times hotter than usual." So, they were thrown in. After some period of time, the king looked in, and out of amazement, he asked his advisors, "Did we not put three men in the furnace? Now I see four." (Paraphrase here). Then the three lads walked out unharmed—not even one hair singed on their heads. As a complete about-face, the king then praised the boys for their faith and promoted them in his province.[1]

This story presents two very important life lessons: Always do the right thing, and know that God is always with you. If you think about it, these two lessons go hand in hand. Doing the right thing oftentimes can be scary and even costly, but knowing that God is right there makes this challenge easier.

I gave a talk about a year ago to some 40 to 50 teenagers at a local youth ministry on this very passage of scripture and these two life lessons they could take away from the passage. I talked about the temptation to use drugs, skip school, or shoplift from a store, all at the behest of some mighty strong peer influence. I assured them that if they truly believed God is always with them, then they would have the power to resist the temptation and not allow the peer criticism to negatively impact how they feel about themselves. I emphasized to them that if they got in the habit of always doing the right thing, always making good decisions and knowing full well God had their backs, then there would be no limit to what they could accomplish.

DO THE RIGHT THING

I am reminded of the story of David and Goliath. In order to protect the Israelite army and secure a victory for them, young David took on the mammoth Philistine giant. No one else dared to take on this challenge except David. He did the right thing in facing this enemy because he knew God was on his side. He never flinched, and he never hesitated. With a slingshot and a stone, he took down this monster of a man.

We as adults can adopt these same principles in our daily lives and use them as guidance when we are faced with difficult decisions to make. Here are some examples that maybe you can relate to:

1. Your daughter is pregnant and initially wants an abortion.[2] She makes the decision on her own to go through with the pregnancy and put the child up for adoption. She made the right decision in saving the life of her child, knowing full well that God would be with her during her emotional healing.

2. You know of a distant relative who needs a kidney transplant, and miraculously, you are the only match. There is one problem though. The doctors have advised you that the risk of the surgery is very high, and there is a strong possibility there could be lifelong complications for you. Without the transplant, the distant relative is sure to die. You make the right decision and go through with the surgery, knowing full well God is going to be with you during surgery and afterwards.

3. A friend of yours offers you an opportunity to go into business with him for a guaranteed huge profit margin, and financially, you need a break. Bills have mounted up, and the risk of foreclosure on your home is high. You learn, however, that this business venture has some areas of questionable legality. You make the right decision, and you tell your friend

thanks, but no thanks, knowing full well God is going to be with you during your financial crisis.

4. Your spouse is the head of the financial department in the company she is employed with. Her boss comes to her and tells her that in order to keep her job, she must alter the "numbers" to make the company appear to be in a better financial position than it actually is. Your spouse makes the right decision and tells her boss, "No!" knowing full well that God is going to be with her every step of the way.

5. You feel that God has laid it on your heart to give up your highly paid and prestigious job and take over a small country church. You are a certified lay speaker in the Methodist church and, therefore, hold the necessary credentials to take on this position. The church can pay only very little in salary and compensation. You only have three years left before you will be fully vested in your retirement at work. You make the right decision and take on that church, knowing full well God is going to provide for the needs of you and your family.

You may find these five examples to be somewhat extreme and think that God would not put you or someone else in these extremely difficult situations. That may very well be true, but the point of all of this is this: Life will present us with challenging situations where we or someone we know will be faced with "doing the right thing." We must be prepared to make that right decision regardless of the consequences, however large or small they may be. We must make the decision that is pleasing to God and that will bring Him honor and glory. We must have the self-assurance that God will be with us. He will always have our backs!

Oh, by the way, did I mention that in my five examples above, there was a fair amount of prayer mixed in before the decision was

DO THE RIGHT THING

made? Oh, yes! Prayer is always an essential component when we are faced with a situation where we must decide whether or not to do the right thing.

Thought: When was the last time you were in a difficult situation and you were called on to do the right thing? Did you pray about it? How did it turn out?

Let us pray: Dear Lord, help me always make the right decisions in my life. In doing so, help me to make prayer an essential part of the process, knowing full well that You will always be with me. Amen.

---

[1] The king was so impressed with their faith that he developed some faith of his own, or did he?

[2] I know the issue of abortion is a hot political topic, and I am not trying to get political in this devotion. But the issue of abortion can invoke some mighty strong Christian principles. Too, adoption holds a very special place in my heart and Gayle's heart. As I told you in my second book, Michael and Kat are both adopted.

Day Twelve

JESUS, OUR ARK

This is the account of Noah and his family. Noah was a righteous man, blameless among the people of his time, and he walked faithfully with God. Noah had three sons: Shem, Ham and Japheth. Now the earth was corrupt in God's sight and was full of violence. God saw how corrupt the earth had become, for all the people on earth had corrupted their ways. So God said to Noah, "I am going to put an end to all people, for the earth is filled with violence because of them. I am surely going to destroy both them and the earth. So make yourself an ark of cypress wood; make rooms in it and coat it with pitch inside and out. This is how you are to build it: The ark is to be three hundred cubits long, fifty cubits wide and thirty cubits high. Make a roof for it, leaving below the roof an opening one cubit high all around. Put a door in the side of the ark and make lower, middle and upper decks. I am going to bring floodwaters on the earth to destroy all life under the heavens, every creature that has the breath of life in it. Everything on earth will perish. But I will establish my covenant with you, and you will enter the ark—you and your sons and your wife and your sons' wives with you. You are to bring into the ark two of all living creatures, male and female, to keep them alive with you. Two of every kind of bird, of every kind of animal and of every kind of creature that moves along the ground will come to you to be kept alive. You are to take every kind of food that is to be eaten and store it away as food for you and for them." Noah did everything just as God commanded him.

—Genesis 6:9–22 NIV

And Noah did all that the Lord commanded him. Noah was six hundred years old when the floodwaters came on the earth. And Noah and his sons and his wife and his sons' wives entered the ark to escape the waters of the flood. Pairs of clean and unclean animals, of birds and of all creatures that move along the ground, male and female, came to Noah and entered the ark, as God had commanded Noah. And after the seven days the floodwaters came on the earth.

—Genesis 7:5–10 NIV

For what I received I passed on to you as of first importance: that Christ died for our sins according to the Scriptures, that he was buried, that he was raised on the third day according to the Scriptures, and that he appeared to Cephas, and then to the Twelve.

—1 Corinthians 15:3–5 NIV

NESTLED AWAY IN A SMALL KENTUCKY TOWN, WILLIAMSTOWN, IS A Christian theme park known as the Ark Encounter. The park opened in 2016 and averages 1.5 to 2 million visitors each year. Gayle and I visited this park in June 2024. The park has a zoo, a virtual reality center, a zip-line,[1] and a huge buffet restaurant capable of sitting 1,500 patrons at one time.[2]

The centerpiece of this theme park is a large replica of Noah's Ark built to the correct dimensions: 510 feet long, 85 feet wide, and 51 feet high. What an amazing sight to behold, outside and inside. This theme park is operated by an organization known as Answers in Genesis, a young-earth creationist organization believing the earth to be only 8,000 years old (give or take) and not millions of years as some scientists proclaim.

After Gayle and I spent around three hours in the Ark, and an additional two hours in the zoo, virtual reality center, and, yes, the buffet, we decided to go to the main auditorium to see if anything was going on, and there was. A contemporary Christian band called True Song was playing, and they were wonderful. Then, we were treated to an hour-long lecture by the creator and CEO of Answers in Genesis, Ken Ham—a prolific author, scientist, and preacher.

After this talk, when we were headed to the buses to leave the park, Gayle and I both realized something at the same time. Despite the massive, impressive, and amazing replica of the Ark and the wonderful surrounding environment, the Ark and the Ark Encounter is simply about the gospel of Jesus. Let's look at some basic comparisons between Noah and the Ark and Jesus:

1. **Ridicule**: While it is not mentioned in scripture, and you may not agree with me, I believe that Noah and his family received a lot of scorn and ridicule from the wicked and violent people of that day. "Noah, what in the world are you building?" "Noah, you say that it is going to rain and that the whole earth will be flooded!" And, "How many animals are you taking?" "Noah, you are crazy! You have lost it!" What about Jesus after he was arrested? He was mocked, spat on, made fun of, and ridiculed. As He hung on the cross, the people hollered out, "If you are the son of God,

save yourself and come down from there."³ Isn't it true that when people do not understand something or even refuse to understand something, they resort to ridicule? So true, definitely for Jesus and maybe for Noah too.

2. **Wood**: The main component for the Ark was wood. The main component for the cross was wood. A lot of wood for the Ark and not so much for the Cross. Noah's Ark saved him and his family, who were the only ones left on earth, and Jesus' cross saved humanity from their sins.

3. **Obedience**: Genesis 6:22 says, "Noah did everything just as God commanded him." Noah was tasked with building a structure the likes of which had never been seen before. He obeyed in spite of the massive responsibility he was tasked with. Noah kept the faith, and he obeyed. We can say that Jesus was the same way. As discussed in Day Four, Jesus, in the garden, begged God to take the cup from Him, but eventually, the human Jesus relented and obeyed. It is like Jesus said, "I trust you Father, and I will obey You and suffer death by the most barbaric means of death known." Jesus kept the faith and obeyed.

4. **Miracles**: Without question, the Ark was a true miracle from God. Not only did it have to be of incredible size, but it also had to withstand the massive waves of the floodwaters crashing against it. We have to remember it was not floating in a lake or even in a choppy ocean. No, it had to float in water reaching the tops of the mountains in the land. That is a miracle. And what about Jesus? He was all about miracles. He never hesitated to cure blindness, bring speech and hearing back to folks, and raise people from the dead. Or what about feeding five thousand plus or

JESUS, OUR ARK

walking on water? Our Jesus was truly the "Miracle Man."

I believe that Jesus is our Ark today, and I have three primary reasons why I believe that:

1. The Ark protected Noah, his family, and the animals from the flood that God brought on the entire earth. Jesus protects us from the floodwaters, the storms and trials that come into our lives. Remember Jesus' infamous words: "Come to me, all who are weary and burdened, and I will give you rest. Take my yoke upon you and learn from me, for I am gentle and humble in heart, and you will find rest for your souls. For my yoke is easy and my burden is light."[4] Jesus is telling us, "Man, I want to help you. Come here!"

2. Noah opened the door to the Ark for his family and animals to enter the safe sanctuary of the Ark.[5] They came in for the Ark's safety and protection. And don't you imagine that those who mocked and ridiculed Noah during the building process were the first ones to bang on the door, pleading to be let in when the floodwaters began to rise. Now with Jesus, He is the door. He told us in His Sermon on the Mount that all we have to do his knock, and He will open the door for us.[6] In other words, Jesus is telling us to enter to find His peace, love, grace, mercy, and salvation.

3. Lastly, the Ark rescued Noah and his family from God's judgment on the world by the great flood. They were protected by their faith in God. Jesus also rescues us from God's judgment of eternal death by our belief in Jesus as our Lord and Savior. Jesus has overcome the floodwaters of death so that we can live eternally with Him in Heaven.

My friends, Jesus is our Ark! He protects us from the storms of life. He protects us from the judgment of death. He opens the door for the forgiveness of our sins and life eternal in Heaven. Thank You, Lord Jesus!

Thought: Have you ever thought about Jesus being our Ark? Has there been a time when He has saved you from a storm or protected you in some way?

Let us pray: Heavenly Father, You protected Noah and his family, and through Your Son, Jesus, You protect me in so many ways. Help me always to look to Jesus as my Ark for safety and protection. Amen.

---

[1] I begged Gayle to let me take a turn on this zip-line, but can you believe she would not let me? Or maybe you do not believe the "begging" part!

[2] And oh yes! We visited this restaurant.

[3] See Matthew 27:38–44 NIV

[4] Matthew 11:28–30 NIV

[5] The Ark's door at the Ark Encounter is at least 20 feet high.

[6] See Matthew 7:7–8 NIV

Day Thirteen

SALVATION LOST?

The Jews who were there gathered around him, saying, "How long will you keep us in suspense? If you are the Messiah, tell us plainly." Jesus answered, "I did tell you, but you do not believe. The works I do in my Father's name testify about me, but you do not believe because you are not my sheep. My sheep listen to my voice; I know them, and they follow me. I give them eternal life, and they shall never perish; no one will snatch them out of my hand. My Father, who has given them to me, is greater than all; no one can snatch them out of my Father's hand. I and the Father are one."

—John 10:24–30 NIV

For God's gifts and his call are irrevocable.

—Romans 11:29 NIV

Forever Me, *Lucy*, and the **Lord**

HAVE YOU EVER LOST ANYTHING? SURE, YOU HAVE. WE ALL HAVE.[1]

I remember one Christmas when my kids were young. My grandmother would always write us a $100 check for my wife and me and our two kids. We were cleaning up, and Gayle and I could not find the check. We knew we received it. We looked everywhere in the house, but no check. Now, $100 is a lot of money today, but it especially was back in the 90s when I was trying to build my practice and Gayle was a young schoolteacher. Where could this check have been? Gayle and I looked at each other, and almost at the same time, we each said, "The garbage can outside!" Oh no, not the garbage can full of messy diapers, food from Christmas celebrations, and no telling what else was in there. Somehow, and I am not sure how, I got elected to take on the task of going through the trash. Well, after about 20 minutes of this utterly unpleasant experience, I found the check.

Over the years, there has been a theological debate over the following question: "Can a person lose his or her salvation?" I have friends who are strong Christians who believe that one can, and I have others, equally as strong in their faith, who say no. Others take a different approach and believe that no one can cause one to lose their salvation, but the person himself or herself can make the decision to turn away.[2] I fall within the "No" camp, and hopefully, I will make a decent case in support of my position.

Reverend W.A. Creswell says that "salvation is instantaneous, absolutely complete and irrevocable."[3] I want to focus on two specific parts of this statement and then tie it back to our passage from the Gospel of John above.

Absolutely Complete: There is nothing left out of or missing in the salvation Jesus gives us. It is by His blood, and His blood alone, that our sins are forgiven. His blood cleanses our ugliness, our selfishness, and our dirtiness all at once. Nothing in this entire world can do it better than Jesus's blood. It is the best cleaner on the market today.

SALVATION LOST?

Irrevocable: God's gift to humanity—Jesus' death on the cross and His resurrection three days later—is not something He will allow to be recalled, revoked, reversed, retracted, changed, or altered. It is a done deal! You can take it to the bank. It is our bond with God that is true and everlasting. As the Romans passage says above, it is a gift. What a wonderful gift it is.

So, let's look at what Jesus says in John 10: "No one will snatch them out of my hand." I want to first focus on the word "snatch." When I think of this word, I immediately conjure in my mind a person who is a pickpocket, someone who has the uncanny, albeit illegal, ability to take something from one's pocket in a split-second, many times without the victim knowing what happened. Or what about the phrase "snatching defeat from the jaws of victory"? This phrase is typically used in the realm of sports when one team is winning, and then in a second, the game quickly turns in favor of the other team. When something is snatched away, not only is it done very quickly, but it is done when a person least expects it. Jesus tells us that "His sheep" cannot and will not be "snatched" out of His hand or the hand of His Father. They will not allow it to happen. One cannot get the jump on Jesus, nor can one pull one over on God.

The second word I want to zoom in on is "perish." Remember in John 10 above, Jesus says, "I give them eternal life, and they shall never perish." Not only can one of Jesus' sheep—a saved person—not be "snatched away," but this person will not "perish." Will not suffer darkness and death. Will not ever be separated from the Father in Heaven. Will not spend eternity in hell.

A saved person is secure in the arms of Jesus. He will not let go. He will not let circumstances make him fall away. Therefore, a person is truly saved: (1) if this person believes in his heart, mind, and being that Jesus came to the world to save; (2) if this person is truly confident that Jesus died on the cross for one reason and one reason only—for the forgiveness of sins, mine and yours; (3) if this person knows for certain that because of the resurrection of Jesus three days later from the tomb, eternal life in Heaven is real and an absolute;

(4) if this person believes that Jesus is one with God. Then, my friends, that person will not nor cannot lose his or her salvation.

Jesus has got this. He is holding us now in His loving arms as His protection and security for us and will most certainly hold us in His loving arms in Heaven. If our mom, dad, or grandparent could really give a hug that was so full of warmth and love, then wait, just wait until we get to Heaven. Jesus is waiting for us! Can I get an amen? Amen!

Thought: Have you ever wondered if you could lose your salvation? How does knowing that your salvation is secure in Christ change the way you live each day?

Let us pray: Dear our Heavenly Father and my loving Jesus, thank You for Your gift of forgiveness and salvation and Your love for me that knows no limits or boundaries. Thank You for helping me feel safe and secure in Your loving arms. Amen.

---

[1] Now my family accuses me of having a file on every document, important paper, or family record in existence. Maybe that is true. I sure do not want to lose anything! "Go ask Dad. I am sure he has a file on it," as my family always says!

[2] Like the old slogan from Burger King commercials, these others believe that God will simply respond, "Have it your way."

[3] W.A. Creswell Library (Date unknown)

Day Fourteen

THE POWER OF WORDS

But I tell you that everyone will have to give account on the day of judgment for every empty word they have spoken. For by your words you will be acquitted, and by your words you will be condemned.

—Matthew 12:36–37 NIV

The one who has knowledge uses words with restraint, and whoever has understanding is even-tempered.

—Proverbs 17:27 NIV

Likewise, the tongue is a small part of the body, but it makes great boasts. Consider what a great forest is set on fire by a small spark. The tongue also is a fire, a world of evil among the parts of the body. It corrupts the whole body, sets the whole course of one's life on fire, and is itself set on fire by hell.

—James 3:5–6 NIV

With the tongue we praise our Lord and Father, and with it we curse human beings, who have been made in God's likeness. Out of the same mouth come praise and cursing. My brothers and sisters, this should not be.

—James 3:9–10 NIV

HAVE YOU EVER HEARD IT SAID THAT "ONCE THE TOOTHPASTE COMES out of the tube, you can never put it back in"? This is so true for the words that come out of our mouths. Once we say something, we cannot take it back. All of us have said things we instantly regretted.

Words are so powerful because of what they create when spoken or written. How about the old saying, "Watch what you say. You may leave the wrong impression." Words can define who we are and what people think of us. Words are powerful, and they can either build up or tear down. They can be weapons of grace or weapons of destruction. They can do much good or much harm.

From our passages for this devotion, we can glean four major points.

First, there are eternal consequences for the words we speak. Ouch! Really? Yes, the passage from Matthew is very clear. I believe that Jesus is telling us that what we say is really a heart issue. Do we have the right motives and attitudes? Is our heart full of compassion and encouragement? When we are standing before Jesus, He is going to remind us of every unkind and careless word we have spoken. But He will remind us of the good things we have spoken as well.

Second, it is often wise to simply not say anything. We speak when really we do not have something good or important to say. Do

THE POWER OF WORDS

you not find it annoying when people just talk and talk, *ad nauseam*,[1] to the point they have either embarrassed themselves or offended someone. It is good to step back and just listen, knowing the right time to say something.

Third, what we say can have a negative impact on ourselves. The tongue, while small, can be deadly. James says it can corrupt the entire body. Think of someone you know whose words are always negative or even to the extent of being vulgar. And you know what—they are miserable. Their life has always been full of pessimism, destruction, and harm. They have allowed their thoughts and words to control their entire being. They have succumbed to the "fire" that has corrupted their entire being. So sad!

Fourth, James points out that we are guilty of practicing what I would call being "two-faced." We praise God, and then in the next breath, we say something wrong or hurtful to someone. James reminds us that we are all made in our Creator's likeness. So, a wrong word to someone is the same as a wrong word to God. This contradictory behavior should not and cannot happen. In any given situation, realizing we are all very sinful people, we should rely on the power of the Holy Spirit to give us the control of our speech that we need.

To finish up this devotional, I am going to offer some things for you and me to think about in what we say and our choice of words:

1. Do we want to please God or please Satan?
2. Do we want to encourage or discourage?
3. Do we want to inspire or demoralize?
4. Do we want to create confidence or doubt?
5. Do we want to create contentment or displeasure?
6. Do we want to cause peace or unrest?
7. Do we want to cause happiness or sadness?
8. Do we want to praise or blame?
9. Do we want to compliment or criticize?
10. Do we want to flatter or belittle?
11. Do we want to bless or condemn?

12. Do we want to celebrate or dishonor?
13. Do we want to comfort or hurt?
14. Do we want to speak the truth or falsehood?

Remember, my friends, we have a powerful weapon in our words to bring about good or bad. Let's always make a difference in someone's life with what we say. Let's honor our God.[2] Let's glorify Him in how we speak to others. Let's show kindness and love to our fellow brethren. Do not ever forget that one kind word can change someone's entire day!

Thought: What can you do to help yourself harness the power of your tongue?

Let us pray: Dear God, please allow Your Holy Spirit to guide and direct me in all that I say so that my words are always pleasing to You and a comfort to others. Amen.

---

[1] To a disgusting or ridiculous degree.

[2] Deuteronomy 23:23 says, "Whatever your lips utter you must be sure to do, because you made your vow freely to the Lord your God with your own mouth" (NIV). We have a responsibility not to say things that bring dishonor to God.

Day Fifteen

SEND ME

Then I heard the voice of the Lord saying, "Whom shall I send? And who will go for us?" And I said, "Here I am. Send me!"

—Isaiah 6:8 NIV

DO YOU REMEMBER IN GRAMMAR SCHOOL[1] WHEN THE TEACHER NEEDED a volunteer to erase the chalkboard[2] or run a note to the principal's office? Thirty eager and willing hands would raise, bodies jumping up and down. "Pick me! Pick me!" The enthusiasm, the willingness, the desire to help and serve was definitely there with those thirty kids. Each one wanted to be picked and hoped to receive the call.[3]

But why is it that so many times when God calls us, we stiff-arm Him with a resounding response: "No way can I do that!" So here is what we are going to do. I am going to discuss four characters in the

Bible whose responses were different. Then, I will land the plane and see how these biblical characters apply to us today.

Isaiah (Isaiah 6)

Isaiah, considered to be the greatest prophet of all time, had just seen the Lord, and he was asked in the above passage who shall the Lord send. Isaiah never hesitated and said, "I am the one." Now, the task for Isaiah was not an easy task. He was to tell the ones who were "God's select people" that they were going to be destroyed because of the way they had been acting against God. Isaiah took on this daunting mission.

Jonah (Jonah 1)

One day, Jonah, while minding his own business,[4] was spoken to by God, and God said, "Jonah, I need you to go to the city of Nineveh and preach to them and get them to repent of their ways and make a change." Jonah responded with something like this: "God, you want me to do what? I cannot do that. Those people are mean and nasty. They will not listen to me." Jonah went in the opposite direction of where God called him.

Saul (Later to Become Paul) (Acts 9)

Saul was a righteous Pharisee who was consumed with rage and bitterness against the people of "The Way," as Christ-followers were known by in that day. He hated Christians and everything they stood for, and he found ways to have them arrested and even killed. He even went to the High Priest in Jerusalem for permission to capture Christians in Damascus, and he received the answer he wanted: "Permission granted." Little did Saul know that God had a little diversion waiting for him. We are told in Acts 9 that as Saul and his entourage were riding along on the road to Damascus, a great light from Heaven surrounded Saul. Now, let's put this "light" into some perspective with three comparisons:

Example One: Was this "light" as bright as the light in a police interrogation room shining directly in the eyes of the suspect? Brighter!

Example Two: Was this "light" as intense as a welder's torch multiplied by a thousand? More intense!

Example Three: Was this light as bright as Clark Griswold's house with Christmas lights overloading the city's electrical system in the classic movie *Christmas Vacation*?[5] Not even close!

The light was so bright and intense it knocked Saul to the ground, and then the infamous words came: "Saul, Saul, why do you persecute me?" Saul then asked, "Who are you, Lord?" The response? "I am Jesus, who you are persecuting. Now go into the city." At that point, Saul gets up but realizes he is blind. Now, this is not recorded in scripture, but Jesus could have added, "I am alive and well, thank you very much. I am resurrected. Saul, I have some serious concerns with you, but the good news is I am going to fix you."

Ananias (Acts 9)

The cool thing about this character is that he is tied into the story above with Saul. Ananias, a disciple of Jesus, had a dream/vision, and God told him to go to the house of Judas on Straight Street and find a man from Tarsus named Saul. In effect, Ananias said, "No! Lord, have you not heard the reports about this guy? Do you not know about the harm he has done to your holy people?" (In other words, "Lord, this is one bad dude! He is another Hitler. I cannot go.") The Lord came back and said, "Saul is now one of my chosen who will proclaim my name to the Gentiles." (See v. 15) Ananias was told to place his hands on Saul's eyes to restore his sight. So, Ananias finally accepted the call.

From these four examples, we have a resounding "Yes" from Isaiah, "No way" from Jonah, a necessary blinding light for Saul, and some godly prodding for Ananias.

So how do we respond when God gives us a call? And He will call us in some form or fashion every day. Do we respond like Isaiah with a big yes? Do we respond like Jonah with a big no? Or will we require a blinding light on the road to Damascus or some forceful encouragement?

When God calls us, I believe what He is really saying is, "I want you to surrender to My will, surrender to Me." Therein lies the rub. Therein lies the problem. Therein lies what we are fearful of. Surrender? Oh, no! Lord, I cannot do away with all my possessions and become a missionary in China. Lord, I am not cut out to go door-to-door and hand out leaflets. Lord, I cannot stop socializing with my friends who are not strong Christians and only hang out with people who go to church three times a week, quote scripture with every other breath, and call everyone Brother Dave or Sister Mary. Now, please understand that I am not making fun of any of the above, nor am I minimizing what God could very well ask each one of us to do. But I believe when God asks us to surrender, He is more inclined to ask us to:

- Accept Jesus as our Lord and Savior;
- Have complete trust in our Heavenly Creator and follow His commands;
- Seek to do His will always.

And then, we need to be more like Isaiah and say, "I am ready. I am here. I am on it," and do away with excuses.

So when God's call is made, go:

- And give more to the Church;
- And work in the local soup kitchen;
- And visit an elderly shut-in from church;
- And forgive someone who has wronged you;
- And spend more time with Him.

SEND ME

God does not want us to ever say, "Here I am, Lord, but send him, send her." No, He does not. God expects—no He demands our obedience, our loyalty, our service.

Remember, it has been said before that God does not want people with ability; He wants people with availability.[6]

Thought: When God comes knocking at your door and says, "Whom shall I send?" what will be your response? Anything keeping you from responding with a yes like Isaiah?

Let us pray: Lord, when You make a call to me, help me to always lay aside all excuses and, with a grateful and humble heart, accept Your call and say to You, "Lord, send me!" Help that to be my response every single time. Amen.

---

[1] For some of us, we need to kick in the memory jets here!

[2] The predecessor to the dry erase board—for you younger folks. (I guess dry-erase boards are rather obsolete too, right?)

[3] I have to tell you another Ford story. Recently, he was picked by his teacher to be the door holder for the other kids in the class. One afternoon, Gayle and I were in the car line waiting for class to dismiss. Ford's class exits one building and goes into another building to be called to be picked up. We watched Ford's class journey about fifty yards between doors. Of course, Ford was at the end of the line as he had held open the exit door. Then, he took off running to get to the front of the line so he could be there to hold open the entrance door. He was moving in between fellow students with the agility of a cat, nearly knocking down a fellow student or two. He was like someone in an airport trying to reach their gate with few minutes to spare. (Remember the O.J. Simpson Hertz Rental commercial). For sure, Ford answered the call.

[4] Probably working on his next prophecy. He was a great prophet in that day.

[5] See Day Twenty-Seven devotion, "Christmas Vacation."

[6] Greg Laurie June 1, 2012, Online Devotion

Day Sixteen

HEAVEN'S DEW

May God give you heaven's dew and earth's richness—an abundance of grain and new wine.

—Genesis 27:28 NIV

The seed will grow well, the vine will yield its fruit, the ground will produce its crops, and the heavens will drop their dew. I will give all these things as an inheritance to the remnant of this people.

—Zechariah 8:12 NIV

So Israel will live in safety; Jacob will dwell secure in a land of grain and new wine, where the heavens drop dew.

—Deuteronomy 33:28 NIV

DO YOU KNOW HOW DEW IS FORMED? DEW RESULTS FROM MOISTURE condensation as warm air mixes with cool night air. Tiny droplets or fine mist blanket the ground and plants.

In the above three passages, dew is associated with plant growth. Back in the Old Testament days in Canaan, oftentimes there was not enough water for plants to grow, especially during the hot summer months. Dew falling at night was a source of water for the crops to grow and mature. So, the dew is a source of life for the crops and plants.

The word "dew" conjures up for me notions of freshness, coolness, and something akin to a breath of fresh air. Then, when you put it with "Heaven," it takes on a whole new meaning completely on a different level. So, the logical conclusion to be made is if the dew comes from Heaven, then God is the source of the dew. I just love this phrase "Heaven's dew." Think about it. Dew is most noticeable in the morning, symbolizing how God's mercies are new every morning. (See Lamentations 3:23). Too, dew appears quietly and gently just like God's presence in our lives.

Let's explore more about Heaven's dew from today's passages.

First, dew is His word. When we abide in His word every day, we realize just how great and awesome our God is. Fresh and rich every day—a source of life for us. His dew is like "living water," as Jesus told the woman at the well. (See John 4:13–14). It sustains us spiritually.

Second, just as the dew causes new plants to grow and have new life with refreshment and nourishment, God will give new life to those of us who are dead in sin. He will allow us to grow and mature in our faith.

Third, Heaven's dew relates to safety. God promised safety to Israel and to Jacob. God will protect us and take care of us.

Fourth, God is like the dew pouring out His grace, blanketing His people with His love and faithfulness. His grace and mercy appear new, early every day, exactly like the dew. Through God's Holy Spirit, we are refreshed and nourished each day. (See John 7:37–39).

HEAVEN'S DEW

Lastly, Heaven's dew is God's blessing on us providing for all of our needs. He showers us with every wonderful gift every single day of our lives.

Take time to reflect on moments when you have experienced Heaven's dew in your life. Don't ever let a day go without thanking our Father in Heaven for His dew—those sweet blessings from above so rich and abundant.

Thought: How has God refreshed your soul recently? In what ways have you seen His dew in your life?

Let us pray: Dear loving Father in Heaven, thank You for Heaven's dew that You shower me with. Your love, grace, and mercy are such wonderful blessings that I do not deserve, but I sure do enjoy them. Thank You for being the awesome God that You are. Amen.

Day Seventeen

THREE CUPS

Jesus went out as usual to the Mount of Olives, and his disciples followed him. On reaching the place, he said to them, "Pray that you will not fall into temptation." He withdrew about a stone's throw beyond them, knelt down and prayed, "Father, if you are willing, take this cup from me; yet not my will, but yours be done."

—Luke 22:39–42 NIV

A third angel followed them and said in a loud voice: "If anyone worships the beast and its image and receives its mark on their forehead or on their hand, they, too, will drink the wine of God's fury, which has been poured full strength into the cup of his wrath.

—Revelation 14:9–10a NIV

I will lift up the cup of salvation and call on the name of the Lord. I will fulfill my vows to the Lord in the presence of all his people.

—Psalm 116:13–14 NIV

When Michael and Kat were young, they gave me a Tervis Tumbler with the words "Best Dad Ever." To this day, I still use it as a coffee cup when I am in the car. Also, over the past few years, Ford has given me coffee cups with the words "Grandpa" and "Best Grandpa," and my favorite is a cup with a picture of both of us at a Clemson ballgame with the words "Best Grandpa Ever." All of these cups are very special to me.

In today's passages, we have three special cups in scripture: the Cup of Pain and Suffering,[1] the Cup of Wrath and Judgment, and the Cup of Salvation. Let's review each cup and see how they are interrelated.

Cup of Pain and Suffering

After the last supper and before Jesus' arrest, He went to the Garden of Gethsemane (on the Mount of Olives) to pray. He brought along three of His disciples—Peter, James, and John.[2] Jesus knew the enormous task He was facing—death on the cross—so He knew He needed to pray. He prayed indeed! He prayed and asked God to take the cup from him. This cup was full of the pain He would suffer from beatings and humiliation before the cross. This cup was full of the unfathomable and excruciating pain Jesus was going to endure while hanging on the cross. This cup held the massive nails that would be driven into His hands and feet to hold Him to the cross. This cup was full of all the sins of all of mankind, past, present, and future. And this cup was full of the separation from His Father in Heaven that He would experience while hanging on the cross. It was an experience that no one would ever want to go through. But we know that our precious Jesus surrendered to this cup and to the will of God. Forgiveness of sins was on the line!

Cup of Wrath and Judgment

Now, I know what you are thinking. Don, how in the world can you say that this cup is special? Wrath, not good. Judgment, not good either. Please let me set the record straight here. God created everything in existence. God is a God of love, grace, and mercy. He hates sin so very much. He expects obedience from us. When we turn from God, when we fail to follow His commands, then there will be consequences. No one can disagree with the basic notion that when one does wrong, there is a price to pay. Look at Adam and Eve in the garden. They ate the apple and sinned against God. So, what happened? No more garden. The people in Noah's day were evil and violent people, as far from God as one could be. The massive flood was the consequence of their sins. During the end of times, there will be judgment for those who continue to fail to place their faith in God and accept Jesus. God is a Holy God, and His holiness demands justice. He is also a God of justice, which allows for grace and mercy, but it also demands judgment.

Once again, God created everything and set the rules in place. Sin will not win out. Sin was defeated by Jesus' death on the cross. Satan will be defeated when judgment is finally placed into motion when Christ returns. Remember this: The Cup of Pain and Suffering and the Cup of Wrath and Judgment allows for the Cup of Salvation to exist. Our sins were forgiven on the cross. When we place our faith in Jesus for His death and ultimate resurrection from the grave, then salvation, eternal salvation, is within our reach.

Cup of Salvation

What a sweet cup this is. This cup rescues us from the Cup of Wrath and Judgment and provides us with the hope of spending eternity in Heaven with our Creator and with our Savior. Not only will we be with Jesus, but we will also have our loved ones there. I do not know to what extent we will know each other, but I have to think that it will be wonderful. We lift up the Cup of Salvation and say, "Thanks be to our God!"

Each of these three cups plays an integral part in God's plan for all mankind. Jesus had to drink from the Cup of Pain and Suffering so His death on the cross would allow forgiveness from of all our sins from our Father in Heaven. This death was essential to show how much God hates sin and how much He wants everyone to come to Him, to love Him, to obey Him, and to bask in His grace. Sadly, there have been and will be many who will not choose Jesus, and that is where God's cup of wrath and judgment will come into play. People are given chance after chance after chance to become one of God's children. He put His Son on the cross because He simply loves you and loves me. But there will be a time when time has run out and God's mighty wrath and judgment will be on full display. Without question, God does not want anyone to follow the beast[3] as we see in our passage in Revelation. He really does not. He really does not want anyone to underestimate His power. It is going to be a sad day, for sure, for some.

But there is hope! There is a cup of salvation for those of us who have placed our faith in God and have accepted Jesus as our Lord and Savior. That is a hope that has no equal.

My coffee cups—special! These three cups—really special!

Thought: How does the Cup of Wrath and Judgment make the Cup of Salvation more precious to you? How does it make you feel that Jesus willingly took the Cup of Pain and Suffering so that you could have the Cup of Salvation?

Let us pray: Jesus, thank You for taking on the Cup of Pain and Suffering by Your death on the cross so that I might receive the Cup of Salvation. Your sacrifice is absolutely amazing! Amen.

THREE CUPS

[1] We took a look at this in the Day Four devotion

[2] Considered to be the inner circle of Jesus

[3] The beast in Revelation is the Antichrist, who is a partner with Satan during the end of times.

Day Eighteen

OPEN INVITATION

When one of those at the table with him heard this, he said to Jesus, "Blessed is the one who will eat at the feast in the kingdom of God." Jesus replied: "A certain man was preparing a great banquet and invited many guests. At the time of the banquet he sent his servant to tell those who had been invited, 'Come, for everything is now ready.' But they all alike began to make excuses. The first said, 'I have just bought a field, and I must go and see it. Please excuse me.' Another said, 'I have just bought five yoke of oxen, and I am on my way to try them out. Please excuse me.' Still another said, 'I just got married, so I can't come.' The servant came back and reported this to his master. Then the owner of the house became angry and ordered his servant, 'Go out quickly into the streets and alleys of the town and bring in the poor, the crippled, and the blind and the lame.' 'Sir,' the servant said, 'what you ordered has been done, but there is still room.' Then the master told his servant, 'Go out into the roads and country lanes and compel them to come in, so that my house will be full. I tell you, not one of those who were invited will get a taste of my banquet.'"

—Luke 14:15–24 NIV

INVITATIONS ARE VERY COMMONPLACE IN OUR LIVES TODAY. WE receive some form of invitation practically every day. They come in all shapes and sizes. Formal or informal. Verbal or written. Simple or not so simple.

Let me throw out some scenarios. Think of a time when you were anticipating an invitation, such as to a wedding, birthday party, or some special event, and when it came—total exhilaration! You really wanted that invitation.

Now, think of a time when you received an invitation and for whatever reason you declined. An invitation to a friend's retirement party or for a family reunion. Then you heard that it was a great event, and you began to feel a little sorry for not accepting the invitation.

Finally, think of a time when you sent in your RSVP, indicating acceptance, but then you did not attend. How did you feel?

With these examples in mind, ask yourself why you accepted and why you declined. Did you accept for the sake of acceptance? Did you accept because the invitation was for something good? Or did you decline because you simply did not have the time or need for what you were being invited to?

Our parable from Luke[1] is a great passage of scripture with eternal implications. Before we dig into the parable itself, let's take a look at what Jesus was doing before He gave this parable. Jesus was at the home of a Pharisee, having a meal. Probably finished dinner and was maybe having coffee and a dessert.[2] Jesus and those gathered there were talking, and hopefully, they were taking in some of His wisdom. Jesus told them not to take the front seats of honor when coming into a banquet or a feast but to go to the back. Also, He told them when inviting people, invite those who are poor and crippled—those who are unable to repay with an invitation of their own. Then, someone in the group, and probably it was one of those Jewish religious leaders, blurted out, "Blessed is the one who will eat at the feast in the kingdom of God" (v. 15). As this guy spoke this, I am sure he was sticking out his chest in a proud and arrogant fashion, knowing for sure he was guaranteed a place in Heaven. My guess is this guy had too much false confidence in his future.

Let's take a look at this parable and see if we can relate to it in some fashion. The host is God, and the banquet is the future kingdom in Heaven. The Jewish people of the day pictured their future kingdom as a great feast with the likes of Abraham, Issac, Jacob, and the prophets as honored guests. Now let me stop and say that I love to eat and would be in awe of sitting around the table with those guys breaking bread. I am all in if this is what Heaven is like. Sounds good to me. People were invited with the time and date of the party. All responded with a yes. There was no RSVP indicating a decline.

So, when it was time for the party to begin, the host's servant went around, indicating it was "party time." The parable indicates three people, and I am sure there were many more who gave excuses for not being able to attend. I will let you be the judge of the validity of these excuses. Then the servant reported back to his host that no one was coming. What did the host do? He invited those the Pharisees and self-righteous Jews considered to be unworthy—not as good as them. The poor and the lame and probably some Gentiles and Samaritans who the Jews really did not like. Then Jesus said the sobering statement in verse 24, which reads: "Not one of those who were invited will get a taste of my banquet."

What lessons does this great parable have for us?

1. All things are ready. The food has been cooked, and the feast has been spread out. The invitation is free. In other words, Jesus has done all the work already. He has died on the cross for the forgiveness of our sins,

and God resurrected Him three days later, so our eternal destination is secured. God wants His heavenly house to be filled to the brim and for all to respond with a resounding yes to the greatest invitation we will ever receive.

2. God's invitations do not stop when we are saved. He invites us on a daily basis to enjoy the fruits of His love and grace. He invites us to be more Christ-like with more humility and compassion. He invites us to take care of the needy and poor. He invites us to go out and spread the good news of His gospel. All of these are blessings, and we receive them once we accept Christ.

3. Finally, how do we respond to God's invitation? Do we allow the trappings of this world, our society, and our culture to cause us to make excuses, or when that invitation comes, do we respond, accept, and show up?

God is waiting on our response. He is telling us that He has a great feast, a wonderful banquet just waiting on us. And I am here to tell you the best words that we will ever hear: Once we say "yes," Jesus says to us, "You are home. Come in, my son; come in, my daughter."

Thought: How do you respond to God's invitation to the banquet of salvation? Are there areas in your life where you have made excuses instead of fully embracing His call?

Let us pray: Lord, You are a most loving and gracious God. Your eternal invitation is the greatest invitation that I can ever receive. You have reserved a spot for me in Your eternal home in Heaven. Please remove any excuse that I may have and help me to respond with humble and grateful acceptance. Amen.

OPEN INVITATION

[1] Similar parable in the Gospel of Matthew entitled "The Wedding Feast." In our passage from Luke, it is called "The Great Banquet."

[2] Maybe a little creative license here.

Day Nineteen

WONDEROUS LOVE

This is how God showed his love among us: He sent his one and only Son into the world that we might live through him. This is love: not that we loved God, but that he loved us and sent his Son as an atoning sacrifice for our sins. Dear friends, since God so loved us, we also ought to love one another. No one has ever seen God; but if we love one another, God lives in us and his love is made complete in us.

—1 John 4:9–12 NIV

THERE IS A STORY TOLD OF A CHRISTIAN HAVING A CONVERSATION with a Buddhist who professed that his religion was so much better than the Christian religion because Buddhism was a happy religion with a happy god. He further criticized the Christian faith because it was full of blood, suffering, crucifixion, and death. The next day, the Christian saw a poor man starving on the side of the road, near death. Many walked by without helping the starving man. The Christian walked up to the starving man and got him to his feet, and he pondered whether to take the man before the fat and happy Buddha or lay him at the feet of the One who knows what it is like to be in need and close to death.[1] Yes, Jesus knows, and why he knows is simply because of His wonderous love for us.

Any time you talk about God's love, you must first start off with this foundational principle that God does not just love—He *is* love. He is the embodiment of love. Love originated with God. This truth has to be the main focus for any discussion about God's love.

Let's go back to our scripture passage for this devotional. We have three main points that John talks about: 1. Because of God's love, He sent His only Son into our world; 2. Since God loves us, we should love one another; 3. God lives in us, and we are made complete.

God's love was the driving force for sending His Son into this world of ours. His plan for salvation would not have happened if it weren't for His love for each one of us. Not only did God send Jesus to us to teach, to heal, and to be the "gold standard" of perfection that we are commanded to attempt to emulate, but Jesus was also sent to save us wretched, sinful human beings. Yes, to save! How did God do it? We know His plan. To show how much He hates sin and how much He loves us, He did the unimaginable. He did the unthinkable. He put Jesus, His only Son, on the cross to die. The most barbaric of deaths in the Roman culture of that time. A torture that is beyond our comprehension. Not only did Jesus die that horrible death, but God also watched Him die that horrible death. Why did God do this? He did it out of His wonderous love for us.

So, with His bountiful love for us, God wants us to show love for one another. Jesus said more than once that we should take care of the needy, the elderly, and those sick and oppressed. Those folks who are less fortunate than we are. We should all feel truly blessed.

Let me share a story that many in South Carolina and my hometown of Laurens will certainly remember.[2] On September 27,

2024, at around 6:00 a.m., Hurricane Helene hit the north and northwest sections of South Carolina (including Laurens) as a Category 1 hurricane and devastated the area to the likes we have never seen. The people in western North Carolina were also victimized by this hurricane, and many say it will take years for them to even get close to normal. While Florida, the Gulf Coast states, and the coast of South Carolina are regular victims of these massive storms, we are not used to it here in our neck of the woods in the Upstate of South Carolina or in Western North Carolina.

Here in Laurens, the hurricane caused trees and power lines to fall. Homes were destroyed.[3] Power was out for many days. Drinking water and food were scarce for many. Gasoline pumps were not able to function because there was no power. And probably the worst consequence of this hurricane, according to some, was the loss of internet and cell phone service. But as so often happens, people came together and showed love for one another, whether it was providing food and water, helping a neighbor cut up a tree that had fallen, or, like one business establishment downtown, opening doors for anyone to come in to cool off and have a bottled water or a cup of coffee. It is that love of God that permeates through us to others. That is what is so important and heart-warming.

Finally, in this passage in 1 John, when I read that "God's love lives within us and we are made complete," I think of that great hymn, "What Wonderous Love Is This (For My Soul)".[4] It is God's love that fills our entire being. It is God's love that renews and refreshes us. It is God's love that strengthens our spiritual DNA and makes us more willing to show gratitude, compassion, and forgiveness. God's love puts our souls in just the right place.

Finally, I want to go back for a minute to the chaos surrounding our area after Hurricane Helene. Some people, I am sure, have said and will say, "How can a loving God allow this hurricane to happen, knowing full well what the aftermath of the storm will be?" I am here to tell them that God—before, during, and after the storm—still loved and loves us as much as He did when Jesus went to the cross. How do I know that? Faith, my friends! Now, does my faith give me some crystal ball, allowing me to look into the mind of God to figure out why He allowed this storm? Certainly not! But I do know this—in God's infinite wisdom, there is a reason for everything, which our tiny finite minds will never be able to understand. Maybe, just maybe, this storm led to some of the following:

1. A person or a group of people came to faith in God;
2. A person or a group of people took the opportunity to show God's love, which took on the "domino effect" of others showing God's love;
3. A person or a group of people came to know just how blessed they really are;
4. A person got another person or a group of people in the neighborhood to pray together at the same time every day while the storm's effects remained;[5]
5. A person or a group of people contacted someone they had not talked to in years to check on them and offer help and comfort.

I know some of you may be thinking that these things are rather trivial compared to the effects of Hurricane Helene. Okay, I get it. But know this: Nothing goes unnoticed by God, and when it is good for His kingdom, it is not trivial. God has a plan. God knows what He is doing, for sure. Think about our story at the beginning of this devotion. He knows what suffering is all about. He sent His Son to the cross to suffer that horrible death. He did so because of His great love for us. He meets us at every turn and at every time with His great love for us.

God loves you, Gayle!
God loves you, Michael!
God loves you, Kat!
God loves you, Mandy!
God loves you, Ford!
God loves everyone in our great city of Laurens!

WONDEROUS LOVE

And God loves every reader of this devotion!

Thought: Do you ever worry that when bad things happen, God's love is nowhere to be found? What are some things you can do to ease this worry?

Let us pray: Dear loving Lord, keep me ever mindful that Your love for me is bountiful and never ceasing. When I tend to doubt Your love and worry it has gone, bring me back to reality, to the one thing that is ever-constant — You love me and will not stop loving me. Also, help me to take Your love and love those around me. Thank You, Lord. Amen.

---

[1] Source unknown

[2] I am writing this devotion on September 29, 2024, with the benefit of a generator.

[3] Oftentimes, humor is a welcome relief in times of trouble. Gayle and I had a metal open shed pancaked by two fallen trees striking fatal blows about 30 minutes apart. Part of what we stored under this shed were wheelbarrows. Thanks to these two trees, our wheelbarrows were goners. We had a lot of fallen limbs, leaves, and other yard trash in the yard to pick up, but how? We had no wheelbarrows. How could we take this yard debris to the end of the road where we normally place this stuff for eventual city pick-up? Okay, Gayle got creative. She got an old stroller of Ford's out of the garage that she used so frequently when he was younger to stroll him all over town. The stroller was her wheelbarrow, and she took load after load of yard trash to the end of the street. What a sight to behold!

[4] Hymn No. 292, *United Methodist Hymnal*, Harm. 1955, Renewed 1983, Augsburg Publishing House. There are some great verses in this hymn. One in particular: "What wonderous love is this that caused the Lord of bliss to bear the dreadful curse for my soul."

[5] And we know how much God wants prayer from His children.

Day Twenty

IT AIN'T THAT HARD

"He himself bore our sins" in his body on the cross, so that we might die to sins and live for righteousness; "by his wounds you have been healed."

—1 Peter 2:24 NIV

HAVE YOU EVER HAD SOMEONE SAY TO YOU, "IT AIN'T THAT HARD?" In other words, you're making a task or endeavor a lot harder than it actually is. Among my many imperfections,[1] I am without a doubt "technologically challenged." Growing up in the twentieth century, we did not have any of the electronic gadgets, computers, and scientific wizardry that we have today. Ford was able to use a cell phone without breaking a sweat when he was a toddler. Whereas I am trying to master the art of putting airline tickets in my wallet on my phone before we take a trip next summer.[2] I am just amazed at young people today who are able to face challenges and master a task with ease and without worry. So, like with technology, you may hear someone say, "It ain't that hard," when you are reluctant to take something on or are struggling with it.

The opposite mindset is when this statement, "It ain't that hard," is made and someone says it with full confidence in their ability to master what is in front of them.[3] They take it on and do it without a problem, fearless and anxiety-free.

When you look at it, the gospel of Jesus is just not that hard. It is just not that hard to understand, even though some make it out to be very hard to understand. Let me ask this question: Do you like checklists? I know I do. It makes things a lot easier. To set forth a pathway to an understanding of the gospel of Jesus and an understanding of how salvation works, I am going to present a point-by-point and step-by-step process for all of this. Please keep in mind there are no tests, no initiation ritual, and not even a secret handshake. It is very basic, so here we go:

Point One: We are sinful people and separated from God and in need of saving.

Point Two: God sent His only Son, Jesus, to die a horrible death on the cross so that all our sins—past, present, and future—would be forever forgiven.

Point Three: After Jesus died on the cross, He was placed in a tomb that held His body full of death. But God's plan was not finished, so three days later, death was defeated. Jesus rose, alive and as strong as ever. His resurrection from the grave allows us to also be resurrected from death and live eternally with our Creator and Savior in Heaven. Our death is not our final outcome but is just the beginning. We now have life ever after for all eternity.

Point Four: For forgiveness to take hold, we must repent of our sins and seek a change in our lives. What in the world does it mean to repent? It means to be truly and sincerely remorseful, contrite, and sorrowful for our wrongs against God's holy nature, coupled with a true change in behavior.

IT AIN'T THAT HARD

Point Five: Salvation comes simply by the love and grace of God. God loves us very much, and it is by His favor that we do not earn or deserve it. He offers this gift of salvation to everyone who accepts.

Recap: It is the grace of God and the blood and cross of Jesus—that is it, and that is enough. The gospel is all about God's plan, and Jesus carries out that plan. Now that "ain't so hard," is it? Go on and accept Jesus as your Lord and Savior.

I want to close with two quotes similar in nature, one from a well-known minister and one from a friend:

> We must effectively step over Jesus to get to hell. (Greg Laurie, Harvest Ministries, Riverdale, California)

> The cross is located just outside the door to hell. (Sam Hunter, 721 Ministries, Greenville, South Carolina)

God wants everyone to be saved, and He will give us chance after chance to accept what Jesus has done for us on the cross. If this acceptance is not made, then the very last second before going to hell, the last opportunity is there to see Jesus and the cross. One last opportunity to be saved.

I hope you have it now!

Thought: Have you ever struggled with understanding how or why Jesus saved you? If so, what might have caused that difficulty?

Let us pray: Lord, thank You for loving me so very much that You would save me through the death and suffering of Your Son, Jesus. And then bringing Your Son, Jesus, back to life so eternity is a reality for me. Help me never to forget what You and Jesus have done for me Amen.

[1] I wonder why in my devotional books I seem to have a compelling need to admit to these.

[2] I am writing this devotion in October 2024. Is 10 months enough time to learn? I sure hope so!

[3] Day Seven devotion "Giving Up Control:" Remember, I talked about teaching my kids to drive, and they would say, "I got this, Dad." They were also thinking, *This driving ... it ain't that hard.*

Day Twenty-One

GOD'S FAMILY

For this reason I kneel before the Father, from whom every family in Heaven and on earth derives its name. I pray that out of his glorious riches he may strengthen you with power through his Spirit in your inner being, so that Christ may dwell in your hearts through faith. And I pray that you, being rooted and established in love, may have power, together with all the Lord's holy people, to grasp how wide and long and high and deep is the love of Christ, and to know this love that surpasses knowledge—that you may be filled to the measure of all the fullness of God. Now to him who is able to do immeasurably more than all we ask or imagine, according to his power that is at work within us, to him be glory in the church and in Christ Jesus throughout all generations, for ever and ever! Amen.

—Ephesians 3:14–21 NIV

WE ALL BELONG TO FAMILIES. YES, I SAID FAMILIES, PLURAL. CERTAINLY, our family of a spouse, children, parents, and brothers and sisters would be what we think of as family. But we belong to other families. Our church family is a very important one. While the following are probably better known as groups or associations, what about our family of co-workers, our family of friends, or our family of people who share common affinities and interests? While all of these families are good and so very important, they are all temporal. But God's family is both natural, permanent, and eternal. It is the everlasting family.

We are going to look closely at Paul's letter to the church in Ephesus and the wonderful benefits that are associated with this family.

We gain strength through God's Holy Spirit.

I had an entire devotional on the Holy Spirit of God in my second devotional book, *Still Me, Lucy, and the Lord*. When one becomes a true believer in Jesus, God's Holy Spirit takes up residence in our very being. The Holy Spirit provides the power, the guidance, and the direction for us to navigate through good times and bad times. When we are faced with a challenge or difficult situation, we have the strength to overcome and survive.

When hope seems lost, the Holy Spirit refocuses our attention on what is truly important in our lives—that hope of eternity in Heaven. It is that hope of eternity that binds together the members of God's family.

We have Christ's indwelling in our hearts.

With Christ within us, we strive to become more like Him. We are called to strive for perfection—the perfection found only in Christ. We all want to be more loving, more compassionate, and more in tune with the needs of others. In the Day Nineteen devotion, I talked about Hurricane Helene, which hit parts of South Carolina and North Carolina. I talked about the many acts of love and kindness shown to others in need. I continue to be in awe of the continuous stories of the many acts of kindness, help, and compassion that to this day (many weeks after Helene hit) are going on in every impacted area. This is what it is all about. Do you want to be more like Jesus? Do I want to be more like Jesus? The answer is a resounding yes!

We are connected with other believers.

Oh, I have said it so many times that we cannot do life alone. And we cannot live out our faith alone. What a wonderful thing it is to be with others, reading scripture, praying, or singing hymns. Those of us who are believers have all experienced "mountain-top spiritual experiences." I would wager a guess that most of these experiences were with others in one setting or another. Whether it was a Bible study, a worship service, or just a few people gathered outside in the cool of God's day, praying, it was a great experience. Without question, we need each other. We can be formidable in times of need. Connecting with other believers, in or out of church settings, is an important part of life. We should always strive to become closer with our spiritual family each and every day.

We have a God who has no limit.

Our heavenly Father has no limits. Having that full and complete awareness that God is all-powerful and has no limits is so important. Just knowing that the leader of this family is able to do anything and everything, know anything and everything, and accomplish anything and everything is very reassuring and comforting. I know when I was young, growing up, there was nothing my dad could not do, and he knew everything, especially when it came to sports. Having full confidence in any leader simply strengthens the group.

Having that full confidence in God also strengthens the family—God's family.

Okay! Are you a part of God's family? If not, do you want to be a part of God's family? I sincerely hope there will be a big ol' yes!

Thought: Have you ever thought about God's family being the ultimate family to belong to? How does knowing that you are a part of the ultimate family of God change the way you live your daily life?

Let us pray: Lord, You are the Creator and Sustainer of all life and all that there is. You have simply paved the way for everyone to be a part of Your wonderful family—God's family. Thank You for such an honor and privilege. Amen.

Day Twenty-Two

LIVING IN A SECULAR WORLD

Therefore, I urge you, brothers and sisters, in view of God's mercy, to offer your bodies as a living sacrifice, holy and pleasing to God—this is your true and proper worship. Do not conform to the pattern of this world, but be transformed by the renewing of your mind. Then you will be able to test and approve what God's will is—his good, pleasing and perfect will.

—Romans 12:1–2 NIV

Am I now trying to win the approval of human beings, or of God? Or am I trying to please people? If I were still trying to please people, I would not be a servant of Christ. I want you to know, brothers and sisters, that the gospel I preached is not of human origin. I did not receive it from any man, nor was I taught it; rather, I received it by revelation from Jesus Christ.

—Galatians 1:10–12 NIV

Do you know the first story of secularism in the Bible? It is when Moses walked down the mountain with the Ten Commandments and saw the Israelites worshiping a golden calf they had made. Now, do you know how Moses responded? He said, "Holy cow!"
Please do not allow this cheesy joke to prevent you from continuing to read.

For purposes of this devotion, we are going to simply define "secular" as "non-religious." But let me be clear that not everything secular is a bad thing. Something being non-religious does not automatically put it in the negative column. No, our world offers us many great things. Wonders of nature, amazing technology, the arts, and the list goes on. But there is a bad side of our secular world that will be the focus of this devotion. The seriousness of this continues to get worse every day. The bad side of our secular world is when it contradicts Jesus and His truth.

Our modern society and culture in which we live provide so many challenges for a Christian in his or her walk with the Lord. The bombardment of what our world offers provides a daily test of our faith. Someone who is a non-believer is also prey to this barrage of secular misdeeds, and secularism (with the help of Satan) has seriously affected the mindset, values, and morals of many people.

Paul Zuckerman, in his 2014 book *Living the Secular Life: New Answers to Old Questions*, gives some alarming statistics, and I will share a few:

LIVING IN A SECULAR WORLD

1. The number of people claiming no religion ("nones") was well below 10% in the 1990s, but increased to 20–30% of the American population by 2010.

2. Thirty to fifty percent of the "nones" claim to be atheist or agnostic.

3. Ninety percent of those identified as secularists claim to have no interest in any religious pursuits.

So, problem number one with secularism is that people are turning away from God in record numbers. Just look at the state of our churches. And I bet if that survey was done today, the above percentages would be higher. People do not consider a relationship with Jesus to be important. I have even heard people say that the Bible is not that important. Too hard to understand. Just another archaic piece of history that does not apply to our society today. Oh, how sad it is for people who refuse to accept God's Word, which is alive and, contrary to what they think, is so relevant to us today.

What is important, and herein lies problem number two, is the secular world has promoted "Self" to be the controlling factor on how we live. It is all about "Me," and the world will give me more because I deserve it. I am a good person, and I work hard, so why not get my fair share of the pie? Our culture has drilled into us that we should go for whatever makes us happy. We are entitled to experience life in any way we want. Oh, how sad again. How sad is it that so many refuse to believe that everyone is sinful and in need of a Savior who can provide more than just happiness but so much joy and hope.

Then, our world allows us to accept whatever truths we want. What I consider as "true" is for me to decide, and you can't tell me what is truth. You have your "truth," and I have mine, and by golly, you better accept mine, or you are intolerant. If you do not tolerate and accept how I live, how I think, how I feel, how I express myself, then you are an intolerant bigot. And for sure, do not even mention to me any religious or faith-based ideas because chances are it will contradict my "truth" and what I believe. Hence, problem number three. Once again, how sad.[1] The truth of God is the only real truth there is, and it trumps my truth, your truth, and their truth.

I believe that the fourth problem—and there are many more—has been going on for a long time, and it is this: Prayer has been, is, and will continue to be under extreme attack. Prayer is fundamental to our Christian faith, and any believer reading this devotion can attest to the fact that prayer works! Many times, we see prayer heal the sick, mend the struggle, lessen the anxiety, and provide so much positive energy to a situation that the results are just mind-boggling. I am such a big advocate of prayer, and I just love being around a prayer-warrior who can offer to God such a warm, sincere, and uplifting prayer. Just warms my heart. But prayer is not welcomed in so many facets of our society. The notion of prayer is trampled on at every turn. So sad, sad, sad.

Now, since we have identified some of the problems with our secular world and culture, how can Christians live, survive, and thrive in this world we live in? I do not have any magic answers, nor will these ideas automatically change the world in one grand swoop. These are just some practical, simple ways we can react when our secular world throws a punch.

1. *Trust in God when times are so uncertain.* Truly know that God has this. God is in control. He will continue to guide and protect. There is absolutely nothing out of His reach. Remember what we are told in Proverbs 3:5–6: "Trust in the Lord with all your heart and lean not on your own understanding; in all your ways submit to him, and he will make your paths straight" (NIV).

2. *Remember Jesus has already been through this.* The great thing about Jesus living on this earth for 33 years is that He has experienced a lot of what we experience, so He is able to relate. He said in John 15:18–19, "If the world hates you, keep in mind that it hated me

first. If you belonged to the world, it would love you as its own. As it is, you do not belong to the world, but I have chosen you out of the world. That is why the world hates you" (NIV).

3. *Accept Jesus as your rock and protection in your storms of life.* There is no better protection than that which Jesus can give. When you are mocked and ridiculed for your faith, remember Jesus offers us another promise. We again find in the Gospel of John, where He says, "Peace I leave with you; my peace I give to you. I do not give to you as the world gives. Do not let your hearts be troubled and do not be afraid" (John 14:27 NIV). His peace does not offer the absence of conflict, but it does offer the ability to thrive and persevere in times of conflict. Get into His Word so you can stand on its truth. Think through life with a lens of the Bible by knowing Bible verses and principles. There are so many benefits to doing this.

4. *Pray.* The most effective weapon we have is prayer. We should pray for strength in times of secular upheaval. We should pray for strength in times when our faith is shaken. When sin mounts a mighty attack, we should pray for Paul's Armor of God as found in his letter to the Ephesians.[2] But our prayers do not stop with us. We should pray for those non-believers who persecute believers, who mock and scorn us, and those who hold utter contempt for our beliefs. Pray that God will turn them from their non-holy, secular ways towards Him. Pray that God will give them a new mindset in life. Pray that their hardened hearts will melt when they truly hear the name Jesus.

We have a strong opposition against us, and their beliefs are as strong as our beliefs, but their beliefs are simply wrong and full of folly. Allow me to end this devotion with a story. One day, an atheist professed to his friends that "if there is a God, then I am going to beg Him right now to come down and strike me dead at the very spot I stand." Well, nothing happened, and the atheist said, "See!" So his request begs the question: Why would our Lord in Heaven, our Creator and Sustainer of all life and this universe in which we live take the time to come to earth and kill this atheist? He would have no reason to and certainly would not want to. Our Lord in Heaven is patient, and He is waiting on this atheist to come to his senses and become a believer in faith. God wants everyone to be saved.

Thought: What can you do to counter the effects of this secular world? How can you strengthen your prayer life?

Let us pray: Our Father in Heaven, You give me the assurance that You are in control, and as bad as our world becomes sometimes, I can still have Your peace. That is so satisfying and comforting. Amen.

---

[1] Please indulge me and allow me to share something I just heard. I am finishing up this devotion on October 22, 2024. I learned that this past October 17, 2024, a political candidate was holding a rally, and two college students in attendance hollered out, "Christ is King" and "Jesus is Lord!" While what was said may have arguably not been appropriate for a political rally, the candidate responded in an absolutely horrible way. This candidate said, "You guys are at the wrong rally." That is bad in and of itself. But the candidate's response fueled others in attendance to mock, heckle, and even physically assault these two young students before they left the rally. And then to add the proverbial "salt to the wound," this same candidate, several days later, took the campaign to a church.

[2] Ephesians 6

Day Twenty-Three

DEATH (AND THEN THERE IS GRACE)

For just as the Father raises the dead and gives them life, even so the Son gives life to whom he is pleased to give it... Very truly I tell you, whoever hears my word and believes him who sent me has eternal life and will not be judged but has crossed over from death to life

—John 5:21, 24 NIV

SOME OF YOU MAY BE WONDERING WHY I AM DOING ANOTHER DEVOTION on death. The first devotion is entitled "Victory," and I discuss how we can proclaim our victory over death. In this devotion, I want to approach death from a different angle. Why? Because the concept of death is so very important for building a strong foundation in a

Christian's faith walk. We must understand that death is not just the cessation of life but a conversion to a different state of being.

Let me start by saying that anything I say in this devotion should not be construed by the reader to mean that I believe death is anything less than a very tragic event in anyone's life. I have lost both of my parents, both in-laws, and my only sibling—my brother. All were somewhat expected due to age or health, but each day it happened was still a very, very sad day. I miss all of them very much. But what about the accidental deaths of children or young people? How heartbreaking and painful those deaths are to those parents and those close to the victims. Those tragic events just tear at the very fiber of the family's being. I am reminded of Gayles still-to-this-day very close college roommate. She and her husband lost their twin boys at a young age in separate tragic accidents years apart. Watching them grieve and suffer was so hard to do. But their faith and resilience kept them going even in the midst of many horrible days and sleepless nights.

The point in all of this is that when I suggest that death to a believer is not the last nail in the proverbial coffin or that death should not be worried about, I am not attempting to paint a rosy picture of death. But hopefully, by the end of this devotion, we can see death from a new perspective—one that considers both the experience of the deceased and the impact on those left behind. A different attitude about death, if you will.

Benjamin Franklin once wrote that "Nothing is certain but death and taxes." I take exception to this statement. First of all, taxes are nothing to some folks because they never pay any. Enough said. As to death, here is where the challenge begins. Once again, however, I will take exception to this part of Franklin's quote, and I believe my exception will be clear as we go through this devotion.

I want to address death from the position of a non-believer and from the position of a believer.[1] A non-believer, sadly, does not accept the absolute fact that Jesus died on the cross for the forgiveness of our sins (because we all are sinners and in need of forgiveness). Furthermore, a non-believer does not recognize the fact that God

DEATH (AND THEN THERE IS GRACE)

brought His Son, Jesus, back to life three days later. That tomb Jesus was in was big-time empty on that Sunday. Why do people not accept the cross and resurrection? I have said many times that non-believers are willing to accept the fact that when they die, that is it. End of existence—no more. The problem is they have no understanding of God's grace.

I cannot accept the fact that in God's infinite wisdom, He created human beings for life on this earth, no matter how short or long, only for their existence to end there. I believe that God took some time in planning and creating each one of us. I do not see why God would not offer each one of us the option of living after our physical death. Some people are willing to treat death as some great finale to their lives. They are willing to post the sign "The End" at the end of their life. They are willing to accept the fact that death has won. We believers do not! Again, God's grace is not within a non-believer's mindset.

I have great news, and this is the great news that all believers have. There is more after our physical deaths. Someone once said that death is the canker sore on all our worldly plans and joys. While there may be some truth to that statement, death is by no means a "canker sore" on our heavenly plans and joys. Because Jesus died on the cross and forgave us our sins, we are washed with His blood. When we appear before Him in Heaven, we will be in a clean and holy state. Otherwise, we would never be able to step foot into Heaven as utterly sinful creatures. Part two of God's plan is just as remarkable as part one is with the cross. God brought Jesus back to life three days after His horrible death on the cross. That resurrection allows for life eternal in Heaven. Death does not have the final say. Death is not the end of our existence. There is no "The End" sign at our grave. Eternal life is only possible because of God's wonderful grace and mercy. We die physically and are either buried in the ground or cremated. Then there is God's grace. Because of His great love for us, He extends to us His grace so that we can continue to live and live with Him for all eternity. God's grace to the rescue!

We as believers have that absolute assurance and hope that when we die, we will be with Jesus in Heaven. For those who are left behind when a loved one or close person dies, while it is still sad, they can rejoice knowing that this loved one or close person is with Jesus.

Hallelujah and thank You, Jesus!

Thought: How does the hope of eternal life impact your view of death?

Let us pray: Lord, Your plan for the redemption of the human race and the salvation of our souls is absolutely amazing. It is all because of Your wonderful grace and mercy. Thank You for Your love. Amen.

---

[1] There is another situation of a "no death" experience, and you can read about it in Day Eighteen in *Still Me, Lucy, and the Lord*. That devotion is entitled "The Rapture."

Day Twenty-Four

OUR AMAZING GOD

Ask now about the former days, long before your time, from the day God created human beings on the earth; ask from one end of the heavens to the other. Has anything so great as this ever happened, or has anything like it ever been heard of? Has any other people heard the voice of God speaking out of fire, as you have, and lived? Has any god ever tried to take for himself one nation out of another nation, by testings, by signs and wonders, by war, by a mighty hand and an outstretched arm, or by great and awesome deeds, like all the things the Lord your God did for you in Egypt before your very eyes? You were shown these things so that you might know that the Lord is God; besides him there is no other. From heaven he made you hear his voice to discipline you. On earth he showed you his great fire, and you heard his words from out of the fire. Because he loved your ancestors and chose their descendants after them, he brought you out of Egypt by his Presence and his great strength, to drive out before you nations greater and stronger than you and to bring you into their land to give it to you for your inheritance, as it is today. Acknowledge and take to heart this day that the Lord is God in heaven above and on the earth below. There is no other. Keep his decrees and commands, which I am giving you today, so that it may go well with you and your children after you and that you may live long in the land the Lord your God gives you for all time.

—Deuteronomy 4:32–40 NIV

THERE ARE MANY MYSTERIES IN LIFE. THINGS THAT ARE SIMPLY HARD TO wrap our minds around. Here is a list I have come up with, and maybe you have wondered about some of these too.:

1. Why does the school grading system use A, B, C, D, and F, but no E? Where is the E?

2. Why do they make hotel luggage carts so hard to maneuver? There's no way to make a 90-degree turn with one of those.

3. When we know full well that the batteries are dead, why do we still press the buttons on a television remote harder?

4. Why does the dentist talk with us knowing we cannot respond with all the dental equipment inside our mouths?

5. Why do people tattoo their faces?

6. Why are chicken fingers called chicken fingers when we know that chickens do not have fingers?

7. Why is it that when you are in Walmart, you don't know anyone? (At least, that is the case for me.)

OUR AMAZING GOD

The above examples were just for fun. Seriously, my friends, the greatest of all mysteries is the mystery of our amazing God. God has been referred to as an "impenetrable mystery."[1] God possesses so many attributes and characteristics that are mind-boggling. "How was He able to create the world and all of mankind?" "I can't believe He knows every thought of every person on earth every single minute of every day." And, according to Luke 12:7, He knows the number of hairs on the heads of everyone! Wow! What miracles! When you sit down and really think about God, many of the miracles like these examples fly around in your mind. At least, they do in my mind. There is no way I can even come close to being able to discuss all of God's amazing traits, so I am going to limit my discussion to three attributes. Please understand that I am placing no greater significance on these three than any others. They are all equally important and, again, so absolutely amazing.

God Is Infinite Without Origin

While all of God's attributes are hard to understand, this one may very well top the list. The fact that God has always existed and was created by no one or no thing and has no limits or boundaries is just so hard to grasp. American pastor and author A.W. Tozer writes this about the infinite nature of God:

> To admit that there is One who lies beyond us, who exists outside of all of our categories, who will not be dismissed with a name, who will not appear before the bar of our reason, nor submit to our curious inquiries; this requires a great deal of humility, more than most of us possess, so we save face by thinking God down to our level, or at least down to where we can manage Him.[2]

Oh, how hard we try to figure God out. We put Him in a box of our reasoning and place limits on Him so we can, as Tozer said, "manage Him."

The folly of our thinking. We are finite beings subject to finite time and space. God is not. He is the direct opposite. We were created, and He was not. This is so important for us to know because He is the Creator, and we are His creation.

So how do we worship our amazing, infinite God? We must first humble ourselves. Then, we revere Him. We remain in constant awe of Him. Give Him all honor and praise. Finally, we must keep the following passage on our hearts and in our minds: "Great is our Lord and mighty in power; his understanding has no limit."[3]

God Is Faithful

Think about this: We humans are sinful people. We too often fail to obey God. We disappoint Him. But God remains faithful despite our many shortcomings. The Apostle Paul makes a great observation when he said, "If we are faithless, he remains faithful, for he cannot disown himself."[4]

Another man by the name of A.W., A.W. Pink, English Bible teacher and author, wrote, "God is true. His word of promise is sure. In all His relations with His people, God is faithful. He may safely be relied on. This is the basis of our confidence in Him."[5]

I remember the time when I was hitting brick wall after brick wall trying for a particular employment position. God reassured me that in time, it would come and encouraged me to exercise some patience and trust in Him. It came, and for sure, God kept His promise. It is so reassuring that God will never change His mind nor renege on a promise, and His love never lessens for us. This gives us hope. This gives us peace.

God Is Holy

What does holy mean? Sacred, divine, saintly. With any definition of holy, there has to be extreme and ultimate perfection associated with it.

OUR AMAZING GOD

Pastor and author John MacArthur talks about God's holiness this way:

> Of all the attributes of God, holiness is the one that most uniquely describes Him and in reality is a summation of all His other attributes. The word holiness refers to His separateness, His otherness, the fact that He is unlike any other being. It indicates His complete and infinite perfection. Holiness is the attribute of God that binds all the others together.[6]

God is perfect 100% of the time, and His perfection requires us to strive towards perfection. Jesus tells us, "Be perfect, therefore, as your heavenly Father is perfect."[7]

Certainly, we will never reach perfection, but God's standard requires us to earnestly try. God's holy character is perfectly balanced—perfect in all of His ways.

So there you have it. Three attributes of God—He is infinite, He is faithful, and He is holy. What an amazing God we have. Let's all live a God-saturated life. Why not? With all the wonderful characteristics God has, there should never be any hesitation.

Thought: When have you seen God's faithfulness in your life? How does God's holiness affect the way you live?

Let us pray: You are an amazing God I have. You are perfect in every way and faithful at every turn. You have no limits and are able to do exceedingly great things. Keep me ever mindful that You are the Creator and Sustainer of all life existing before time began. Help me to remain in awe of You as I serve You and praise Your holy name. Amen.

[1] Christianity.com, accessed 7/22/21

[2] A.W. Tozer, *The Knowledge of the Holy*

[3] Psalm 147:5 NIV

[4] 2 Timothy 2:13 NIV

[5] A.W. Pink. *The Attributes of God*. Accessed April 9, 2025. https://www.reformedreader.org/aog02.htm.

[6] "God's Holiness." Grace Quotes. Accessed April 9, 2025. https://gracequotes.org/topic/god-holiness/

[7] Matthew 5:48

Day Twenty-Five

THY WILL BE DONE

Teach me to do your will, for you are my God; may your good Spirit lead me on level ground.

—Psalm 143:10 NIV

This is the confidence we have in approaching God: that if we ask anything according to his will, he hears us.

—1 John 5:14 NIV

Now may the God of peace, who through the blood of the eternal covenant brought back from the dead our Lord Jesus, that great Shepherd of the sheep, equip you with everything good for doing his will, and may he work in us what is pleasing to him, through Jesus Christ, to whom be glory for ever and ever. Amen.

—Hebrews 13:20–21 NIV

> *Whoever does God's will is my brother and sister and mother.*
>
> —Mark 3:35 NIV

GROWING UP, MY PARENTS WOULD JOKINGLY SAY, "DON'T DO AS I DO; do as I say."[1] Now, if a parent were serious in making this statement to a child, it would be some misguided parenting. I believe we would all agree with that. What the statement means is, "My actions do not align with what I say, so follow what I say and not what I do."

With God, however, His parenting phrase would be, "Do as I do and also do as I say." I believe our response to Him should be what I titled in this devotional: "Thy Will be Done." I could have easily titled this devotional, "We Will Do Your Will."

Let me start off by saying this: Doing God's will should be our immediate default reaction to everything in our lives. Now that I have said this, I know what your question is going to be. How do we know what God's will is in every situation we encounter in our lives? That is a great question that I have struggled with and everyone else has struggled with over the years. It is simply hard to know every time what God expects of us—what will align with His will.

So I am going to share some practical points that we can use in learning God's will for our lives.

First, we must develop the mindset that God's will is perfect, timely, and far superior to our will. Listen, we need to remove from our tiny, finite brains that we somehow can solve a situation that we are in—or make a decision about something we are facing—just as well as, or even better than, God can. That is the wrong way to think. God is a whole lot smarter than we are. He created this entire universe and everything in it. We are simply no match for God on any given level.

Second, with the right heart, we must humble ourselves. We must have the full realization that we are sinners, and without God in our lives, we are simply no better than those pesky Pharisees[2] that Jesus had to deal with during his ministry here on earth.

Once we have our minds and hearts right, where do we go from there?

Next, we must have a relationship with our Heavenly Father. The great thing about this is that He wants to have a relationship with us, and so from our end, we must foster a relationship with Him. As with any relationship, the more time we spend together, the stronger the relationship becomes. We do this with regular prayer time with God. We simply ask God to reveal His will to us at a time and in a manner He believes to be best. Seek His guidance through His Holy Spirit to learn what His will is in any given situation. One may ask why we pray for His will to be done when His will will be done anyway. We do that so we can learn to conform to His will.

Then, after prayer, we need to have a steady and intentional diet of His Word. Reading, studying, and meditating on scripture will help us learn what God's will is. Just look at what God has done in scripture and the many actions He has taken and promises He has made. Let's look at a few.

Actions

Jonah 1–4: Jonah tried to run away from God's plan for Jonah to preach to the wicked town of Ninevah. When Jonah repented and embraced his mission, God gave him another opportunity to go to Ninevah. God's will is a will of second chances for everyone. (I talked about Jonah in a prior devotion)

John 3: God sent His only Son, Jesus, to this world to save us. God's will is to save everyone.

John 18, 21: Peter denied knowing Jesus three times leading up to Jesus' crucifixion. After the resurrection, Jesus and Peter talked, and what a wonderful conversation of forgiveness and restoration they had. God's will is to restore everyone.

Acts 9: God took the hater of Christians, Saul (later to become Paul), and turned him into a great man of faith on the Road to Damascus. God's will is to transform everyone. (Also, I talked about Paul in the same devotion).

Promises

Deuteronomy 31:8: God promises us He will never leave us or forsake us. God's will is for us to have peace in Him.

Isaiah 41:10: God promises us He will give us strength when we are afraid. God's will is for us to be courageous.

Matthew 11:28–29: Jesus promises us we can always come to Him when we are weary and burdened, and He will give us rest. God's will is for us to take comfort in Him.

John 16:33: Jesus promised His disciples, and He promises us, that He has overcome the world, so we should take heart. God's will is for us to never doubt.

Once we develop a humble mindset and establish and maintain our relationship with God through reading His Word and regular prayer time, then we are on our way to learn God's will for us. What do we do once we know His will? We need to have that unwavering trust—that confident expectation that God's will, once again, is perfect and complete. We must believe that the outcome of any given situation in our lives, even before it comes about, is the right outcome. Evidence of this trust is when we thank Him for the outcome, even when we do not have any idea what that outcome will be. That is trust, my friends.

We must be patient. Oh, we are creatures that want it now. We do not have time to wait. If it does not come right now, then I will lose out on what I so desperately want or need. No, we need to step back, take a deep breath, and be patient. Pray to God for this patience. It will be worth the wait, for sure.

THY WILL BE DONE

Last, we need to have (and I love this word) tenacity. We need to be tenacious[3] about seeking to find and do God's will in our lives. Being tenacious means being persistent and relentless in this endeavor. Never give up on this most essential quest in our faith journeys.

Yes, God, Your will be done. Done every single minute of our lives.

Thought: Is finding God's will hard for you? What helps you to try and find it? Which of the practical steps I have shared are you going to try and implement?

Let us pray: Dear Lord, help me to be tenacious in seeking to find Your will in my life. Help me to realize the importance of this and help me to further realize that I need Your guidance and direction from Your Holy Spirit. Your will be done, Lord. Your will be done. Amen.

---

[1] Comes from an old English proverb.

[2] Jewish religious leaders who Jesus constantly referred to as hypocrites. I have mentioned these Pharisees several times in my devotionals. I love how Jesus handled them.

[3] More about my family. For both of my kids, sports was a regular thing in their early age through teenage years. For Michael, I can remember when he was a senior in high school, he played on the line in football. One game, he bummed up his knee pretty bad. Given the fact that there were not many "extras" on the football team at the private school he attended, he stayed in the game and played the rest of the game on the gimpy knee. A great example of tenacity! For Kat, she played on the girls' basketball team at this same private school, and she was more of a defensive player than one draining three-pointers in the net. For her, it did not bother her to dive on the floor for a loose ball or even dive into the stands for the ball after a wayward pass. Another great example of tenacity!

Day Twenty-Six

I CAN ONLY IMAGINE

> *Therefore anyone who sets aside one of the least of these commands and teaches others accordingly will be called least in the kingdom of heaven, but whoever practices and teaches these commands will be called great in the kingdom of heaven.*
>
> —Matthew 5:19 NIV

I BELIEVE, WITHOUT A DOUBT—HANDS DOWN—THE BEST CONTEMPOrary Christian song ever recorded is "I Can Only Imagine," written and sung by Bart Millard, lead singer of the group known as MercyMe.[1] This song depicts one person's idea of what Heaven may be like by questioning his ability to stand, speak and even his ability to dance for Jesus. But in this fantastic song, it is repeated throughout that he will be "surrounded by Your glory." Oh, I like that. If nothing else, we can be assured that God's glory will be on full display in Heaven, 24/7.

While we do not have a lot to go on about what Heaven[2] will be like, we do have scriptures that gives us some clues about what we believers will experience when we arrive at Heaven's door. I am going to cover some of these passages (paraphrased) and then, with some creative license, offer some of my thoughts and ideas of what lies ahead.

John 14:2: Jesus told His disciples, and us, that His Father's house has many rooms and that He is going ahead of all of us to make all necessary preparations. What does this tell us? Heaven is going to be massive and large enough to hold a lot of people. Also, if Jesus is in charge of the preparations, then without a doubt, Heaven is going to be fabulous.

Luke 13:29: Jesus tells us that people will come from all over and from many places and take a seat at the *feast*[3] in God's kingdom. Throughout scripture, numerous references to feasts, banquets, and wedding celebrations can be found. The mood will be festive and joyous.

Revelation 7:16: We are told that there will no longer be hunger and thirst. Once again, a lot of celebration with food and drink.

Revelation 21:4: We are told that no longer will there be tears, death, mourning, crying, or pain. Simply stated, we are going to experience a feeling unlike anything we've ever had before. "Feeling great" does not come close to describing our mental and physical state of being in Heaven.

Revelation 22:5: There will be no need for light sources there, neither lamps nor the sun. Why? Because the light that God will radiate will be more than sufficient.

Luke 23:43: Jesus told the thief on the cross next to Him that he would be with Him that day in Paradise. What does the word paradise mean to you? The dictionary says, "A state of bliss and delight." Something so beautiful and amazing. Something akin to what Adam and Eve experienced in the Garden of Eden before the Fall. More beautiful than any beautiful place on the face of this earth.

I CAN ONLY IMAGINE

Philippians 3:20–21: Paul tells us that when we take up residence in Heaven, our human bodies will become like Jesus' glorious body. Man, our broken-down, frail bodies, full of corruption and disease, will be no longer. We are going to have a new body that will never die and perish.

As I said, with some creative license, I am going to mention my own personal beliefs of what Heaven will be like or, better stated, what I hope it will be like. Before I do, however, I want to put in a disclaimer. Heaven will be more than my small human brain can comprehend now. Nor am I in any way putting myself on the same playing field as God who is the Creator of the eternal home of Heaven. But I really do not think He minds me or anyone else trying to speculate on some of the wonderful things we may experience.

So, here we go!

1. There will be constant worship of God our Father. See Revelation 4:8–9. Some people have said if that is all there is—a constant worship service—then that is going to get boring. No, I am here to tell you that the worship service in Heaven will be nothing like we have ever experienced here on earth. Think of a time when you were in a worship service that was so meaningful and beautiful that your praise for God was, as they say, "off the charts." Well, multiply that experience by a thousand, a million, a billion, a trillion, and maybe, just maybe, you will have slightly scratched the service of what we will experience in Heaven.

2. Scripture says there will be constant celebrating with food, drink, and socializing around a banquet table. This table will be so large we will be unable to see to the other end. Imagine sitting around this table with the likes of the Apostle Paul; Peter, one of the 12 disciples; Abraham, the father of all nations; and the celebrity list goes on. Being able to talk with them and

ask them questions is just going to be simply amazing. To top it all off again, at the head of the table will be our Lord and Savior, Jesus Christ. Just being in His presence alone will simply be more than sufficient.

3. How great will it be to be with those loved ones and friends who were believers and have gone on before us? They will be there, and how great it will be to be with them and love on them and just be united with them. Gosh, knowing that I'll get to see my father, mother, brother, and grandparents[4] after all these years simply adds to the hope of eternity that we Christians enjoy.

4. Lastly, we will be in constant awe and amazement, and I would venture a guess that on everyone's faces will be big-ol' smiles beaming from ear to ear.

I want to close this devotion by touching on what was mentioned a few lines above—our hope in eternity. Once we accept Jesus as Lord and Savior, that hope in eternity immediately swells up in our hearts and minds. This hope is the driving force for how Christians live and behave. This hope is what helps us overcome our problems and trials that we face. This hope fuels our efforts to strive towards perfection—the perfection that Jesus displayed while on this earth. This hope in eternity is hope in the truth of eternity.

Heaven is waiting! Are you ready?

Thought: How much do you think about Heaven? Is there one thing that is a constant reminder of how great and wonderful Heaven will be?

Let us pray: Our Father in Heaven, You gave me hope in eternity once I accepted Your Son, Jesus, as my Lord and Savior, recognizing He died on the cross for me and You brought Him back to life three days later. The resurrection of our Lord gives me this hope. Please keep my heart humble and grateful. Amen.

I CAN ONLY IMAGINE

[1] Gayle and I had the opportunity, along with some friends, to see MercyMe perform live several years ago. Now, I am more on the conservative side when showing praise to God with bodily movements. But I am here to tell you when they performed "I Can Only Imagine," my hands were raised in honor and praise for our Heavenly Father the entire song. What a moment!

[2] The Book of Revelation tells us in Chapter 21 there will be a new Heaven and a new Earth after Jesus' return and the 1,000 year reign. My discussion about Heaven in this devotion will be in general terms, whether before or after Jesus' return.

[3] We will talk more about eating later on in this devotion.

[4] Since there will be feasts and banquets, then there must be a lot of cooking in Heaven. My grandmother, affectionately known a "Clarkie," was a great cook and baker. I hope that I will be able to get some of her chicken and dumplings, along with a chocolate pie for dessert.

Day Twenty-Seven

THE ULTIMATE GIFT

While they were there, the time came for the baby to be born, and she gave birth to her firstborn, a son. She wrapped him in cloths and placed him in a manger, because there was no guest room available for them.

—Luke 2:6–7 NIV

For God so loved the world that he gave his one and only Son, that whoever believes in him shall not perish but have eternal life.

—John 3:16 NIV

IN THE 1989 COMEDY MOVIE *CHRISTMAS VACATION*,[1] CLARK GRISWOLD anxiously awaits the coming of his Christmas bonus. So confident that he is going to receive a rather large bonus, he goes ahead and makes a down payment on an in-ground swimming pool. Each day he waits for the mail to come, but no bonus check. It is not until Christmas Eve that a delivery boy knocks at the door with an envelope. *It has arrived*, Clark thinks. Before opening the envelope, Clark confesses to his family about the swimming pool. With heightened expectations and anticipation, Clark opens the envelope only to find a gift certificate from the Jelly of the Month Club. In an effort to comfort Clark, thick-headed cousin Eddie says "Clark, this is the gift that keeps on giving!"

Even better than a gift from a jelly-of-the-month club is the gift of Jesus. What a wonderful gift He is! He is the best gift ever given in the history of mankind. He is, by far, the ultimate gift. Why is He the ultimate gift? I have four great reasons. 1. He is a priceless gift. 2. He is the gift, as cousin Eddie says, that keeps on giving. 3. He is the gift of God's redemptive plan for mankind. 4. He is a gift that evidences God's love for His children. Let's unpack these reasons.

Most things in our lives carry a price. They have some tangible value. You can say it is worth this much or that much. But there are also some things that have an inestimable worth, such as the blessings in our lives, family, good health, friendships, and the list goes on. But with Jesus, there is no close second. The gift of Jesus is simply too valuable to place a price on. He has a value beyond all price.

Second, the gift of Jesus keeps on giving. We have daily comfort, peace, and rest in Jesus. Jesus gave us the promise[2] in Matthew 11:28–30 that when we are weary and carrying heavy burdens, we come to Him, and He will give us rest. We can go to Him as often as we need to. We have Jesus' promise of friendship found in John 15:14. We have His promise that He will always be with us even "to the end of the age" as we find in Matthew 28:20. Jesus promises "living water" that will lead to eternal life in John 4:13–15. Jesus' promises are endless and true. We have the gift of Jesus that never ends or runs out.

Third, God's plan, His perfect plan, is for the redemption of mankind through the death of Jesus on the cross. God knew from the very beginning that the creatures He created were full of sin and

THE ULTIMATE GIFT

needed forgiveness. Without Jesus dying on the cross and coming alive three days later, we would be doomed. There would be no eternal salvation without Jesus' death and resurrection. But God knew exactly what He was doing. His perfect plan was put together and implemented without flaw or imperfection.

Lastly, the gift of Jesus is simply the best way for God to show His amazing love for us. He loved us so much that He gave up His only Son to die that horrible death on the cross. Have you ever bought a gift for someone, and you could not wait to give that present to that person? You were so excited about the gift and seeing that person open it. I believe, in God's sovereign and divine way, He was like that with Jesus' birth. So elated, so excited to give us the gift of Jesus.

But you know also in God's own sovereign and divine way, it may have saddened Him in some way too. Kinda bittersweet. We know that in Jesus' incarnation, total divinity took on total man. But as the Father laid His precious little baby in that makeshift crib in the manger, something like this may have been said: "There you go, little buddy. You are going to do wonderful things for My kingdom on earth. But in due time, you will learn what you and I have to do. It will be a hard time for you but also for Me. It is going to break my heart to see you like that. I know, and you will learn, how necessary it will be to accomplish my plan for grace and forgiveness. Remember, I will always love You and am so very proud of You." There is no better showing of love and compassion for us than God sending Jesus to earth for the salvation of the world.

We daily need to offer God a full heart of worship, adoration, and thanksgiving. We daily need to focus on celebrating the miracle of the incarnation of Jesus. We daily need to not be like the innkeeper at Christmas but always have a room for Jesus in our hearts. We daily need to celebrate the gift of Jesus and share Him with others.

The ultimate gift of Jesus! The gift that keeps on giving! Thank you, God, and thank you, Jesus!

Thought: What does the gift of Jesus mean to you? How will you celebrate this gift?

Let us pray: Our Father in Heaven, thank You so much for Your ultimate gift of Your Son, Jesus. He is truly the gift that keeps on giving. Help me always to share this gift with others. Amen.

---

[1] This movie is a family favorite of ours. We typically watch it every Christmas, and we laugh like it is our first time seeing it. A great movie! The movie is the third in National Lampoon's vacation series. Written by John Hughes and distributed by Warner Brothers Pictures.

[2] See Day Twenty-Five devotion. Reference to same passage in Matthew.

Day Twenty-Eight

TRUST IN THE LORD

While they were still talking about this, Jesus himself stood among them and said to them, "Peace be with you." They were startled and frightened, thinking they saw a ghost. He said to them, "Why are you troubled, and why do doubts rise in your minds? Look at my hands and my feet. It is I myself! Touch me and see; a ghost does not have flesh and bones, as you see I have." When he had said this, he showed them his hands and feet. And while they still did not believe it because of joy and amazement, he asked them, "Do you have anything here to eat?" They gave him a piece of broiled fish, and he took it and ate it in their presence. He said to them, "This is what I told you while I was still with you: Everything must be fulfilled that is written about me in the Law of Moses, the Prophets and the Psalms." Then he opened their minds so they could understand the Scriptures. He told them, "This is what is written: The Messiah will suffer and rise from the dead on the third day, and repentance for the forgiveness of sins will be preached in his name to all nations, beginning at Jerusalem. You are witnesses of these things. I am going to send you what my Father has promised; but stay in the city until you have been clothed with power from on high."

—Luke 24:36–49 NIV

WOULD YOU HAVE LIKED TO HAVE BEEN THE PROVERBIAL "FLY ON THE wall" and seen the faces of the disciples when Jesus first appeared to them after His resurrection? Can you imagine how they felt? Luke tells us they were frightened and had troubled minds. They were experiencing a bunch of doubt. Then came some joy and amazement. Their heads were spinning, to say the least. Then came an opening of their minds by Jesus, and the doubt was gone. No more fear. Now some faith, some trust, was coming back.

I want to approach this devotion from two different angles on this principle of trust. I will open up our discussion on the first angle with a question. Why do we make it so difficult sometimes to trust in the Lord? The answer is that we do not have that confidence in what we have been taught. Scripture is full of teachings that God should be trusted in all situations. One of my favorite passages from the Book of Proverbs is, "Trust in the Lord with all your heart and lean not on your own understanding; in all your ways submit to him, and he will make your paths straight" (Prov. 3:5–6 NIV). Our sovereign God of all creation tells us and teaches us that He will straighten our paths. He will make things right. He will get us over that terrible hump that is standing in the way of any joy and happiness.

There is a story told about an impala, a type of antelope, who had been raised in captivity in a zoo. Now, impalas have tremendous physical abilities. They can run up to 56 mph, jump 13 feet high and 30 feet in distance. At the zoo, their enclosure railing is only five feet high, yet they do not jump out. Why? Because they do not know what their abilities are. They have not been taught what is on the other side. They simply refuse to take that leap of faith, if you will. The disciples themselves spent three years with Jesus, and He taught them so many things. But when Jesus came to them after His resurrection, they would not take that leap of faith. No, they did not rely on what they had been taught and knew about Jesus when He appeared to them.

For us, we have also been taught so many examples of what our Lord is capable of doing. We need to always remind ourselves that God is the Creator and Sustainer of all life. He is all-knowing and all-powerful. He has told us that and has promised us that. We do not want to be like the impala or the disciples. We should always take that leap of faith and trust in our Lord every time.

Our second angle begins with Jesus doing the remarkable in our story. He asks the disciples, "Hey, anything to eat around here?" In some strange way, this notion of food was the symbol that tied Jesus and His disciples together.[1] The disciples then realized that the group was back. The band was back together with Jesus. Their leader, their coach, was alive and well.

Remember, before His arrest, He told His disciples the Holy Spirit would be coming (see John 15:26–27), and He reminds them of this again in today's passage. What is so special about this story is that, in a powerful way, the emphasis is put on community and togetherness. We cannot do God's work nor grow in faith and trust without others. Certainly, personal time with the Lord is so very important, which I do every day. Time spent with the Lord with other people is so important as well.

Here is what we need to do to maintain that strong trust in God. Stay grounded in scripture so that we are constantly reminded of what He has told us and promised us and then do it regularly with others. We need encouragement from God and from other believers. Now, that is a good combination!

Thought: What areas of your life are you lacking trust in God? How can you begin to build your trust in Him?

Let us pray: Father God, You are all-knowing and all-powerful. You created this entire universe in a mere six days. You created me and others. You brought back Jesus from the dead. Help me to always be reminded of these things as my trust in You is shaken at times. Help me to be reminded that no situation is beyond Your reach. Never let me doubt Your tremendous love for me. Amen.

---

[1] Remember the feeding of the 5,000 in Mark 6:30–44 and The Last Supper in Luke 22:7–20.

Day Twenty-Nine

THE JOY OF A RELATIONSHIP WITH JESUS

The Lord has done great things for us, and we are filled with joy.
—*Psalm 126:3* NIV

ONCE THERE WAS A MAN WHO HAD IT ALL—OR SO HE THOUGHT. A POWerful job, great wealth, a large house with a swimming pool, a beautiful family, dogs, and a membership to the local country club. One evening, before going to bed, he decided that the next day he was going to celebrate everything he had. As he was falling asleep, the only things on his mind were the things he had and how he was going to further enjoy them. During the night, in his sleep, he died.

What went wrong? What did this man fail to have? He did not have a relationship with Jesus.

For those reading this devotion who already have a relationship with Jesus, my response is, "Wonderful and praise God!" Enjoy your joy that only He can provide. Jesus said,

> As the Father has loved me, so have I loved you. Now remain in my love. If you keep my commands, you will remain in my love, just as I have kept my Father's commands and remain in his love. I have told you this so that my joy may be in you and that your joy may be complete. (John 15:9–11 NIV)

This joy is deeply rooted in our very being. It is not the happiness we experience when something good or fun comes our way. While there is nothing wrong with being happy, it is only temporary and only lasts for a short period of time. Man, I am happy when I am watching a good football game, but after about three hours, when the game ends, then I am onto something else.[1] Or, as I have mentioned in another devotion, I love a good steak. But after consuming the steak, my happiness tends to end, especially if I need to adjust my belt.

But joy in Jesus is a totally different game altogether. It is lasting. It is permanent. It is filling. The joy is simply real.[2] What are some of the joys that we experience when we have a relationship with Jesus? For those who have a relationship with Jesus, maybe you will be able to relate to some of the joys we're about to look at, and you can probably make a list of your own. For those who do not have a relationship with Jesus, then some of what I mention might be enticing enough to cause you to want to check Jesus out. Here are some joys:

Joy of Salvation: "Though you have not seen him, you love him; and even though you do not see him now, you believe in him and are filled with an inexpressible and glorious joy" (1 Pet. 1:8 NIV). Knowing that there is eternal life after death in a relationship with

THE JOY OF A RELATIONSHIP WITH JESUS

Jesus brings us joy. As Peter says, it is an "inexpressible and glorious joy."

Joy of Forgiveness: "If we confess our sins, he is faithful and just and will forgive us our sins and purify us from all unrighteousness" (1 John 1:9 NIV). The first step in being saved is the recognition that we are sinners and, without Jesus, we will remain sinners. God does not want anyone in His Heaven to be full of unforgiven sin. We need to be cleaned up by Jesus, and He is the only one to do it. What joy it is to be scrubbed clean by Jesus!

Joy of Unconditional Love: "But God demonstrates his own love for us in this: While we were still sinners, Christ died for us" (Rom. 5:8 NIV). One thing I knew when I was growing up, and even as an adult, was that my parents loved me unconditionally. For Michael and Kat, it was the same growing up, and it remains true today—they trust that Gayle and I unconditionally love them.[3] Unconditional love is so comforting and reassuring. But the unconditional love from our Heavenly Father and Jesus, our Lord and Savior, is a love off the charts. No one's love can come close to matching it. The cross is the evidence of this love. What joy this brings.

Joy of His Presence: "You make known to me the path of life; you will fill me with joy in your presence, with eternal pleasures at your right hand" (Ps. 16:11 NIV). Simply knowing that Jesus is right there with you 24/7 will bring a smile to your face and joy in your heart.

Please understand this: Jesus wants to have a relationship with us. It has been said, "What is amazing is that the Savior of the world would desire a few minutes with me this morning."[4] And if the truth be known, I bet—no, I know—He will give us more than a few minutes if we simply ask. Just think about it: the Savior of this world within which we live simply wants to hang out with us. Talk with us. Pray for us. Teach us through scripture. Protect us and take care of us. This joy that comes from our relationship with Jesus will not only improve our quality of life in so many ways, but it will also improve our relationship with others—our family, our friends, our neighbors, our co-workers, and our fellow church members. That's a joy worth having.

I want to close this devotion with a quote from one of my favorite Christian authors:

> The joy that comes from Christ is not a joy that is dependent on our circumstances, finances, employment, or relationships. Instead it is a continual, never-ending, constant joy that fills our heart and life as we follow Christ. Because of the resurrection, we are filled with inexpressible joy knowing that because He lives, we will live also.[5]

Being filled to the brim with joy from Jesus! That is by far the best joy ever.

Thought: As a follower of Jesus, do any of these joys resonate with you? Which one, and how does it? Which joy would you like to experience more of and have a greater understanding of?

Let us pray: Dear Jesus, a relationship with You is the best relationship anyone can have. Thank You for wanting a relationship with me and allowing this relationship with You to bring me so much joy in my life. And most importantly, thank You for dying for me and coming alive for me. Amen.

---

[1] Now if it is Clemson beating South Carolina, then my happiness does last somewhat longer. (I know on 11/30/24, there was not much happiness with the outcome of that game.)

[2] Just the other day, I heard an ad on the radio for a "psychics" group that will do a reading and tell you your future. The catch slogan is, and get this-, "Experience the joy of certainty." Oh, come on! Really? Rest assured, my friends, I am not going to call their number. Not the joy I am looking for

[3] And certainly unconditional love for Mandy and Ford!

[4] Author Lysa Terkeurst

[5] Dr. David Jeremiah, March 2, 2024 Devotion: "Season of Hope: Inexpressible Joy."

Day Thirty

LIFE AND LEGACY

You make known to me the path of life; you will fill me with joy in your presence, with eternal pleasures at your right hand.

—Psalm 16:11 NIV

Be very careful, then, how you live—not as unwise but as wise, making the most of every opportunity, because the days are evil.

—Ephesians 5:15–16 NIV

I have been crucified with Christ and I no longer live, but Christ lives in me. The life I now live in the body, I live by faith in the Son of God, who loved me and gave himself for me.

—Galatians 2:20 NIV

Whoever pursues righteousness and love finds life, prosperity and honor.

—Proverbs 21:21 NIV

For, "Whoever would love life and see good days must keep their tongue from evil and their lips from deceitful speech. They must turn from evil and do good; they must seek peace and pursue it."

—1 Peter 3:10–11 NIV

Blessed is the one who perseveres under trial because, having stood the test, that person will receive the crown of life that the Lord has promised to those who love him.

—James 1:12 NIV

AS I WRITE THIS LAST DEVOTION FOR MY THIRD BOOK, I AM INCLINED to reflect on my life. I would imagine this inclination is fueled, at least in part, by my turning 72 just a few days before writing this and also due to the fact that I am retiring from full-time work at the end of 2024. Oh, the adventure of getting older!

Life does pass very quickly, does it not? It seems it passes at a much faster pace the older you get. Billy Graham was once asked what the greatest surprise of his life was, and his short response was this: "The brevity of it." Rev. Graham was so right—life is very short. We are told in scripture that life is like a mist that appears for a little while and then vanishes.[1]

How I am going to structure this devotion is first to share some personal thoughts on living my life and then discuss how we all, no matter our age, should focus on what kind of legacy we are to leave when we are gone. I ask you readers to extend me some grace as I share some of my regrets with you as well as some mighty fine blessings. I hope you will learn from them and be inspired to act or make changes in your lives based upon what I'm about to share.

I regret that I did not spend more time with my father in the last few years of his life. He died at the early age of 73. He battled lung issues for many years, and the last few years of his life, he struggled considerably. He was home most of each day, and I would go see him, but not as often as I should have. Why? Because I was too dang busy building my career and raising a family. I tried to make up for it with my mother, who lived to the age of 90. I saw my mother on a regular basis, brought her lunch for both of us, and called her regularly. But I should have done more with my dad. My dad was too proud to ask for my time, and I am also sure he felt that he did not want to "interfere" with my career and family plans. I sure wish he had. Here is my admonishment to everyone reading this devotion. Spend more time with those important people in your lives—family and friends. Let go of selfishness with your time and generously share it with others. The clock is running.

I regret that I have not spent more time helping those in need. Sure, I have contributed financially to worthy causes, but what I regret the most is that I have not put "boots on the ground" to meet the needs of others. Jesus told us that if we are not helping those in need, it is as if we are not helping him.[2] We need to be intentional and alert to the needs around us, and for each one of us, there are plenty of needs in our own backyard. Remember, the clock is running.

Finally, I regret that I did not come to faith earlier than I did. As I told you in my first book, I was a regular in church, served on committees, and did all the right things so that all my "boxes" were checked. I thought I was good to go. But I realized I was not. God carefully led me for several months until, on February 15, 2011, the realization struck me like a bolt of lightning—I needed more. I needed God in my life and Jesus as my Savior. Oh, what a day! If I had found Jesus way before that day in 2011, then my home would have been filled much more with Jesus when my kids were growing up. There would have been more praying, more Bible reading, and church would have taken on a different meaning for my family. Now, thankfully, Gayle is extremely strong in her faith, and both Michael and Kat are believers, but I truly believe that the family atmosphere, while it was really good, would have been on a much higher playing field. Simply stated, God needs to be the centerpiece in every household. Make Him your household centerpiece. Remember, the clock is running.

While I do have these regrets (and sadly there are more), I can honestly say God has blessed me in so many ways, too many to count. When I pray to God each day, I always include thanksgiving for my blessings, blessings that I do not deserve. I believe it is necessary to always recognize our blessings because they are gifts from God. It is also necessary so that we do not get bogged down with our regrets without focusing on the positive aspects of our blessings.

I have been blessed with a wife who has put up with me for 48½ years, even with all my imperfections, some of which I have shared with you in my devotionals. She is a great cook and a great companion.

I have been blessed with a son who never hesitates to come to the aid of his aging parents to fix things, to put things together, or simply to figure something out that we can't. Gayle, how many times have you or I said, "Need to call Michael?" He never turns us down.

I have been blessed with a daughter who has a tremendous work ethic and has a great sense of humor.

I have been blessed with a daughter-in-law who took the greatest of care of Michael after his tragic fall in August 2023. She did it with so much love and compassion.

I have been blessed with a grandson who is so smart, imaginative, and just so much fun to be around. Too, he is coming around in the faith arena in a mighty way! (Sure, I would love to have more grandchildren, but if he is the only one, then I will still feel blessed beyond measure.)

LIFE AND LEGACY

I have been blessed with a secretary of 26 years who remained loyal and so devoted to me and my work. I could not have done it without her.

I have been blessed with the smartest and most dependable law clerks any judge could have.[3]

I have been blessed with good health for a 72-year-old. I do take a few prescription medicines, and I have had cancer in the past, but taking everything into consideration, I am very fortunate. Maybe a few nights a week at the gym helps a little too.

I have been blessed with great friends, and many of them are strong believers who are a tremendous encouragement to me as I go each day in my walk with the Lord.

I am blessed to have a God who loves me.

Blessings are such an integral part of life. We should always maintain a high level of gratitude, knowing that there is only one source of our blessings, and that source is our Heavenly Father.

As I contemplate the regrets and blessings in my life, my focus also goes to what legacy I want to leave when I die. A good friend of mine said recently, based upon Ecclesiastes 7, "What do we want people to say about us when we die?" This is a great question, and I know that leaving a legacy is very important to him, and it should be to us. What legacy do we want to leave? What positive impact have we made on others? This is something that everyone should think about, young and old. So here are three questions that I would ask each one of you to think about: 1. Do you "walk the talk"? 2. Do you have a mission and vision? 3. Are you making a difference? When you can answer all three in the affirmative, then you are leaving a legacy.

I hope that when I leave this life and go to my next life in Heaven, people will say about me simply three things:

1. I was a man who found life trusting in God.
2. I viewed my life through a lens of humility and gratitude.
3. I had a positive impact on at least a few folks.

May we all live a life overcoming our regrets, enjoying our many blessings, and living a legacy that makes our Lord proud.

Thought: What are your regrets and blessings? What legacy are you leaving?

Let us pray: Lord, I thank You for simply being the amazing God that You are. So full of grace, mercy, and love. I am so grateful for the many blessings You shower on me every day, even in the midst of the regrets I face. Help me and others leave a legacy that is lasting and pleasing to You. And all God's children say, "Amen."

---

[1] See James 4:14.

[2] See Mathew 25:40–46.

[3] Okay! I have finally said what I have done for a living even though many of you already know this. I have been intentional about not mentioning it until now at the end of this my third book for reasons that maybe I will mention at another time.

www.ingramcontent.com/pod-product-compliance
Lightning Source LLC
Chambersburg PA
CBHW022109090426
42743CB00008B/781